4 HUGH BAIRD COLLEGE
BALLIOL ROAD
BOOTLE L20 7EW
TEL: 0151 353 4454

T63079

391.09044

HUD.

Return on or before the last date stamped below.

2/3/11.			
2 4 FEB 2012			

What Every Woman Should Know
Lifestyle Lessons from the 1930s

What Every Woman Should Know
Lifestyle Lessons from the 1930s

Pictures and Facsimile Pages from the
Daily Mail

Christopher and Kirsty Hudson

Edited by Sarah Rickayzen

Trans
Atlantic
Press

Contents

Introduction   7

Cookery   8

Household Hints   28

Fashion   44

Beauty   76

Lifestyle   96

Answers to Correspondents   114

First published in 2008
This edition published by Transatlantic Press in 2010

Transatlantic Press
38 Copthorne Road
Croxley Green, Hertfordshire, WD3 4AQ

A catalogue record for this book is available from the British Library.

ISBN 978-0-9558298-1-9/978-0-907176-62-3

Printed and bound in China

Introduction

THE 1930s are the lost decade. Sandwiched between the Great Depression and World War 2, they have the feeling to us now of an interlude in a tragedy, an uneasy calm between the storms.

In the Soviet Union, the 1930s marked the deep winter of Stalin's Communist dictatorship. In Italy, Mussolini's Fascist regime carried all before it. In Britain, intellectuals divided bitterly between the two extremes, and fought on both sides in the 1936 Spanish Civil War. Meanwhile the growing threat of Adolf Hitler began to overshadow the political scene.

Nevertheless, Britain was at peace. Despite the labour unrest, and Oswald Mosley's ridiculous Blackshirts, 1930s Britain was a haven of political stability. Stanley Baldwin, the leading political figure of the decade, was not impressed by talk of revolution. Given the choice, he preferred to do as little as possible. His stolid, unsmart, middle-class decency was much appreciated by the British public and set the tone of British government.

The Depression, caused by a slump in world prices, lasted until 1933. Wages fell; unemployment hit three million, the highest total ever. Financial help from the government averaged out at about £1.50 per family per week. Living conditions were often squalid: for some families, Sunday lunch consisted solely of potatoes. In November 1932, unemployed men were being paid six shillings a ton for collecting pebbles off a Norfolk beach.

Yet there was another side to this picture of gloom. Despite the Depression, living standards were actually rising. The heavy manufacturing industries, mostly in the north, on which Britain had built its wealth, were losing ground to light industry, mostly situated further south. By 1933 the National Grid had been completed, allowing hydro-electric power to free industry from its dependence on coal and iron. Most towns had their own gasworks, providing light, heat and the power needed to operate labour-saving devices in the factory and in the home.

Meanwhile new synthetic products meant that all kinds of goods could be produced more cheaply. Car tyres could now be made from synthetic rubber. A synthetic resin produced bakelite, the first easily usable plastic, which could be coloured and moulded into any shape. These were the new industries. By 1939, half a million British workers were employed making plastics.

As this book illustrates, the 1930s, for all its forebodings, marked the beginning of the modern era. It ushered in the consumer revolution, in which new industries sprang up to provide goods to the individual consumer. Houses, cars, clothes, presents, new foods - everything from ice-cream to new breakfast cereals - were manufactured by companies who advertised intensively to create a mass market. Telescopic back puffs for backless gowns, portable water softeners, wallets with an attachment to beat pickpockets, a Simnel cake for Mothering Sunday - everything was available, at a price, for the discerning shopper.

And prices were competitive, another novelty. An ABC teashop in 1932 offered a wide range of dishes at one shilling including Fried Fillet of Plaice and Roast Beef and Yorkshire Pudding with Chips. A Baked Apple Dumpling pudding was fourpence, the same as Cauliflower in White Sauce. In poorer districts, a penny or two could be shaved off the price.

Women were the powerhouse of the consumer revolution. They at last had the vote, on equal terms with men, and increasingly they had money to spend, since young women who in earlier decades would have gone into domestic service now went out to work in offices. Their appetite for spending was whetted by a raft of new women's magazines and newspaper sections which instilled the conviction that interior decoration was as changeable a fashion as a summer wardrobe. The new prosperity was fuelled by middle class aspirations. It would take another decade and another World War before the working classes could aspire to join the consumer revolution through the benefits of the Welfare State.

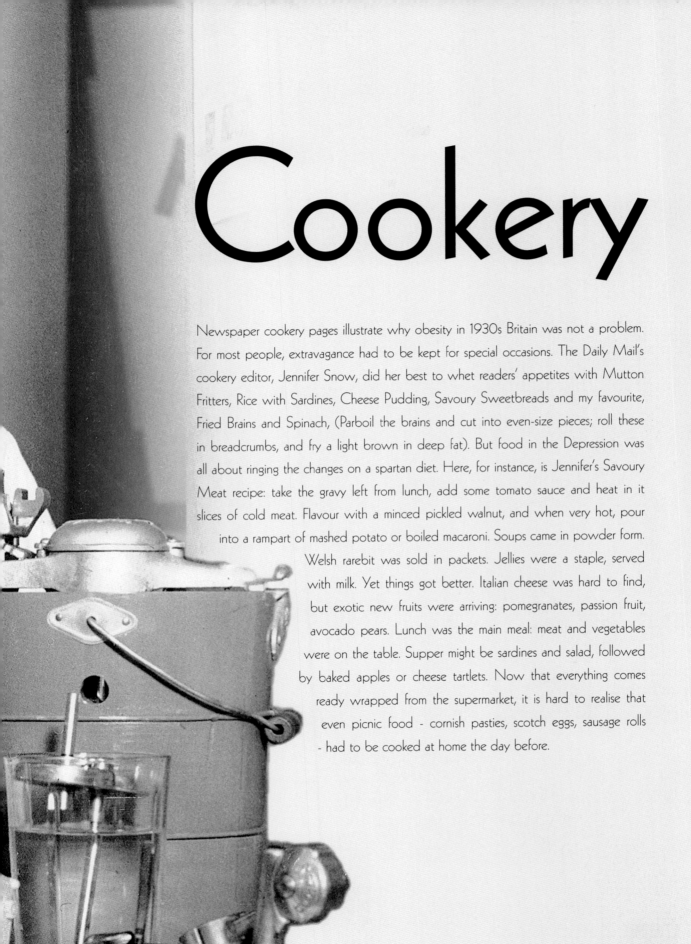

Cookery

Newspaper cookery pages illustrate why obesity in 1930s Britain was not a problem. For most people, extravagance had to be kept for special occasions. The Daily Mail's cookery editor, Jennifer Snow, did her best to whet readers' appetites with Mutton Fritters, Rice with Sardines, Cheese Pudding, Savoury Sweetbreads and my favourite, Fried Brains and Spinach, (Parboil the brains and cut into even-size pieces; roll these in breadcrumbs, and fry a light brown in deep fat). But food in the Depression was all about ringing the changes on a spartan diet. Here, for instance, is Jennifer's Savoury Meat recipe: take the gravy left from lunch, add some tomato sauce and heat in it slices of cold meat. Flavour with a minced pickled walnut, and when very hot, pour into a rampart of mashed potato or boiled macaroni. Soups came in powder form. Welsh rarebit was sold in packets. Jellies were a staple, served with milk. Yet things got better. Italian cheese was hard to find, but exotic new fruits were arriving: pomegranates, passion fruit, avocado pears. Lunch was the main meal: meat and vegetables were on the table. Supper might be sardines and salad, followed by baked apples or cheese tartlets. Now that everything comes ready wrapped from the supermarket, it is hard to realise that even picnic food - cornish pasties, scotch eggs, sausage rolls - had to be cooked at home the day before.

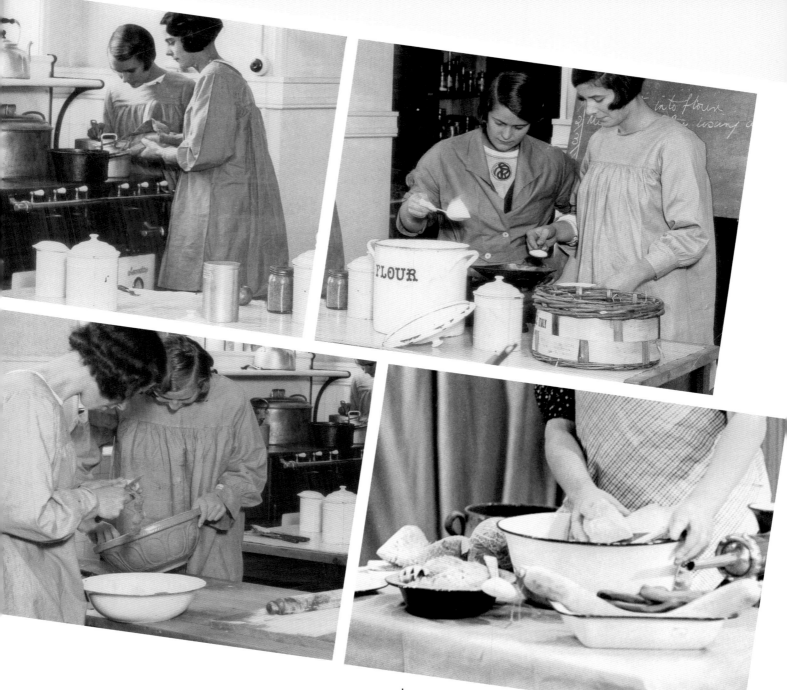

Honey Cakes for Tea

FOR Lemon Honey Cakes cream together 2oz. butter, ¼lb. honey, 1 tablespoonful sugar, 1 egg, juice and grated rind of 1 lemon. Dissolve one small teaspoonful of carbonate of soda in a dessertspoonful of milk, and add. Sift in ½lb. of flour, and beat the mixture well. Half-fill some well-greased patty tins, put into a quick oven, reducing the heat immediately, and bake for nearly a quarter of an hour.

Wholemeal Honey Scones

Mix into a dough 1 breakfastcupful of wholemeal flour, ½ teaspoonful of salt, 1 breakfastcupful of white flour, 2oz. butter, 2 teaspoonfuls baking powder, 2 tablespoonfuls honey dissolved into ½ cup milk. Cut into shape and bake in a quick oven for 10 minutes.

Honey Biscuits

Sift together 2 teacupfuls of self-raising flour and 1 teaspoonful of salt. Add 2oz. of butter. Mix 2 tablespoonfuls of honey in 1 teacupful of milk and add quickly, mixing well. Cut in rounds and bake, serving hot or cold.

Honey Date Strips

You will need 2 eggs, 2 tablespoonfuls of honey, 2 teacupfuls of self-raising flour, 1 teaspoonful of vanilla, 1 teacupful of chopped nuts, 1 teacupful of chopped dates.

Beat the eggs, mix all well together, and put into a long, flat tin, keeping the mixture only ½ inch high. Bake, and cut into strips before serving.

Honey Almond Rolls

Cream ½ teacupful of butter with ½ teacupful of honey. Add the yolks of 2 eggs, 1 teacupful of flour and another of chopped almonds. Mix well, and shape into rolls as thick as a finger. Brush with honey, and bake for 15 minutes in a quick oven.

What You Can Do With SALMON

FRESH salmon is good just now, and chilled Canadian salmon at 1s. 2d.—1s. 4d. is economical, because it goes a long way. Cook it carefully adding the salted water when it has reached boiling point, and letting it simmer, with a little vinegar or white wine in the water, for the time required—ten minutes to the pound and ten minutes over. Tied loosely in muslin it is easy to dish, and if to be served cold it should remain in water until cold.

SERVE hot, with mayonnaise, cucumber, new potatoes and lemon.

Grill in steaks, brushing with olive oil, adding pepper and salt and cooking on oiled greaseproof paper.

Serve cold in bed of lettuce, garnished with watercress, cucumber, mayonnaise, lemon, and sprinkling of red pepper.

Flake and mix with mayonnaise, and serve as hors d'œuvre in small glass cocottes.

Fry steaks of cold salmon, cover with hot vinegar in which have been boiled a little onion, pepper salt, and cloves, and eat cold with cold, well-cooked rice.

Flake, heat with a little tomato sauce, and serve on hot buttered toast.

Flake, and set in aspic jelly, well flavoured. Serve with lettuce.

Mix flaked salmon with lemon juice, chopped gherkin and a little mayonnaise, for sandwich filling.

Make into soup by rubbing flaked flesh through sieve, and adding to good fish stock, mixed with milk and thickened.

Fill baskets cut from cucumbers with flaked fish, mixed with dressing, and serve as appetiser.

FRUITS in PICKLE

By Doris B. Sheridan

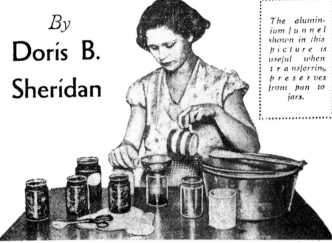

TRY some of these chutneys in sandwiches—if you want to be popular with the family!

THE recent spell of hot weather has given us almost too many plums, pears, damsons, and other early autumn fruits. "We have made jam and jelly," write readers from all parts of the country. "We have done the fruit bottling, and still we have fruits that must not be wasted. What next?" Here are my suggestions.

Plum Chutney

Stone 2lb. plums, stone and chop 1lb. dates, scrape and mince 1lb. carrots, and mince 1lb. cooked beetroot. Put all together into a pan with 1 pint vinegar, and boil until tender. Add ½lb. moist sugar, 1oz. garlic, ½oz. red peppers or chillies, 2oz. ground ginger, and 2oz. salt. Simmer until the mixture is thick and creamy. Divide into clean, warm jars, and seal.

Pickled Plums

Boil for quarter of an hour 2lb. sugar, 1 pint vinegar, and 1oz. stick cinnamon. Wash, dry, and prick with a needle 4lb. plums, and set a few cloves in each. Put the prepared plums, a few at a time, into the liquid, and cook gently until tender. Pack all into clean, warmed jars, fill up with the liquor, and seal securely.

Plum Syrup Without Sugar

For this, bruised or windfall fruit can be used. Wash, wipe, and boil whole fruit in a very little water until soft. Press out all the juice, strain, and boil quickly in an uncovered pan until a thick syrup is formed. Pour into bottles. When cold, cork tightly and cover the corks with melted sealing-wax. Store in a cool, dry place.

Syrups can be made in the same way with pears and apples, the fruit being roughly cut up for the first boiling.

Pickled Damsons

Wash, dry, and prick with a needle 3lb. damsons. Put into a bowl, pour over a pint of vinegar, and leave for 24 hours. Strain, and boil the vinegar with 4lb. loaf sugar, a stick of cinnamon, 3 blades of mace and ½ teaspoonful allspice, and pour again on to the damsons. Leave for 12 hours, then boil all fast for three minutes before turning into clean jars.

Damson Cheese

Wipe sound, ripe damsons and put them into a stone jar or casserole with a lid. Stand the jar in the oven and cook gently until the fruit is soft. Rub through a hair sieve, weigh, and to each pound of pulp allow ¾lb. sugar. Put pulp and sugar into a preserving pan. Stir over gentle heat until the sugar is melted. Stir continuously for three-quarters to one hour until the mixture stiffens. Seal in small jars.

Pear Pickle

Wipe 12 large stewing pears on a cloth, but do not remove the peel. Peel and slice 6 onions. Put the onions and pears, 1½ quarts of vinegar, and 1 teaspoonful of salt into a saucepan. Boil and simmer until the pears are tender but unbroken. Remove these carefully, and unless the onions are soft continue their cooking for a short time longer, and then rub them through a sieve.

Add to the vinegar in the pan ½ teaspoonful cloves, ¼ teaspoonful allspice, 1oz. whole ginger, 1 teaspoonful peppercorns, 3 blades of mace, 1 clove of garlic, 1 teaspoonful bruised mustard seeds, and, if desired, 3 teaspoonfuls tumeric. Boil for 10 minutes, add the sieved onions, and boil for another 10 minutes.

Peel, core, and cut the pears into six or eight pieces each, according to their sizes, and pack them into jars. Strain the vinegar over, divide the spices equally between the jars, and seal.

THAT cold meat pie will be much more interesting if it is served with a good fruit pickle.

Pear Chips

Peel, core, and thinly slice 8lb. pears. Put into a preserving pan with 7lb. sugar, 1 pint water, the chopped contents of a small jar of preserved ginger, and the juice and the finely grated rind of three lemons. Bring all to the boil, and cook until the pears are tender. Pot and seal.

Pears Or Apples In Vinegar

Peel, core, and cut in halves 2lb. small red apples or cooking pears. Boil together for ten minutes 1 pint vinegar, 12 cloves, ¾lb. sugar, and a stick of cinnamon. Put the fruit into the syrup and simmer gently until sufficiently soft to pierce with the head of a pin.

Remove the fruit without breaking, drain, and place in a jar. Boil the syrup until it thickens and reduces, leave until cold, and pour into the jar, making sure that the syrup entirely covers the fruit, then seal.

Crab Apple Pickle

Remove the stems and wipe 3lb. crab apples. Steam until soft. Tie in a muslin bag 1½ teaspoonfuls each of cloves, allspice, black peppers, and ginger. Put into the preserving pan with the apples, 8oz. sugar and 1 pint vinegar. Bring to the boil, simmer for twenty minutes, and turn into warmed jars.

Apple Ketchup

Wipe, peel, core, and cut up 12 sour apples. Put them into a saucepan with boiling water to cover, and simmer until soft. Rub through a sieve and measure the pulp. To each quart of pulp add 8oz. sugar, 1 teaspoonful each of pepper, cloves, and mustard, 2 teaspoonfuls cinnamon, and one tablespoonful salt. Put all into the pan with 2 finely chopped onions and one pint of vinegar. Bring to the boil, and simmer for one hour. Pour into bottles, and seal while hot.

The aluminium funnel shown in this picture is useful when transferring preserves from pan to jars.

HERE ARE TWO FRENCH RECIPES
That Anyone Can Make

POTAGE DE MARRONS AU PETIT SALE FUMEE

Ingredients

A HUNDRED chestnuts, one and a half pounds of streaky bacon, and five pints of water.

Method

Roast the chestnuts and peel carefully, then put them in the water with the bacon, which must be in one piece, not sliced. Boil until the bacon is well cooked. Then taste the soup and add salt if necessary. Pass half of the chestnuts through a fine sieve, the remaining half to be put aside with the bacon. Return the sieved chestnuts to the stock in which they were boiled, and stir until the soup is fairly thick. Arrange the remainder of the chestnuts on a hot dish round the bacon, and serve as the second course following the soup.

This will make a complete meal for four people.

POMMES DE TERRE AU GRATIN

Ingredients

One and a half pounds of minced, left-over meat, chicken, or game, three pounds of potatoes, two chopped onions, a tablespoonful of chopped parsley, some salt and pepper, two eggs, one ounce of Gruyère cheese, and four ounces of cooking butter.

Method

Mince the meat together with chopped onions and parsley, add salt and pepper, and bind with beaten eggs. Boil and mash the potatoes, to which add 2 ounces of butter. Put the minced ingredients in a buttered fireproof dish and smooth over with a fork. Now cover with the mashed potatoes, smooth over, and sprinkle on the grated cheese. Spread over the remainder of the butter, and bake in a hot oven for thirty minutes. The potato crust should then be deep brown. This economical dish, made with left-overs, is enough for six people.

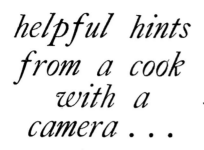

helpful hints from a cook with a camera . . .

in the Christmas Kitchen

ICING THE CAKE YOURSELF?

Then here is the way to set about it. Just let the icing run over the top as you see in the first picture above : it will smooth itself out, and a palette knife dipped in hot water will give the final touch. The sparkling white of royal icing comes chiefly through lengthy stirring, though lemon juice will help further.

And here are some hints about the almond icing. Firm kneading and yet more kneading gives the smooth professional touch to this. It should all be done with the knuckles. Cut a round for the top and a strip for the sides of the cake—it fits better that way—and brushing white of egg over the cake makes the paste stick. A teaspoonful of orange water or rose water to each pound and a half of sugar adds an intriguing flavour.

MINCE PIES

These pies are already figuring in many menus. Brush them with water before dredging them with caster sugar—see picture above—and put them into a fairly hot oven. A brushing with white of egg will make them glossy, but the yolk will give both brown and gloss. Choose which you like—but do let your pastry taste as nice as the filling ! Getting the paste well aerated in the making is more than half the secret of this.

Roast turkey must have its chestnut stuffing, even if the nuts *are* a trouble to prepare. Remove the tops, as shown in the third picture, and bake them for twenty minutes before you can get off the outer and inner skin. Any sieved chestnuts over will make a sauce—a flavouring of lemon and cayenne, please —in case you serve the turkey rechauffé.

THOSE PUDDING BASINS

Basins for Christmas pudding must be really well buttered before they are filled. Have ready a well-buttered round of greaseproof paper for the top. Pudding cloths can now be bought with a tape running round the edge for tying, and a strip of cloth for lifting out of the pot. If you are boiling the puddings and not steaming them, keep the water away from the top. Let the mixture stand for twelve hours before cooking.

BE CAREFUL!

Each ingredient is important for successful Christmas puddings. Flour must be thoroughly dry—warm it if you are not sure——and *sieved* in for lightness, as shown in the photograph above. Weigh or measure *everything*, and put the dry ingredients on pieces of greaseproof paper. Break your eggs separately into a cup before adding to a mixture.

> Cut out this page and keep it : it will be tremendously useful during this month's cooking activities.

ON the AUGUST MENU | TRY THESE RECIPES | *By Pearl Adam*

WHEN a month contains a "Glorious Twelfth" it would never do to talk of its food without mentioning grouse.

But most of us will not get beyond mentioning it for the first few weeks of its sojourn at the poulterer's; and even if we did we should not feel inclined to interfere with the majesty of its presence on our tables other than by roasting it first and then grilling it.

Let it merely be remembered by the lucky housewives who do have grouse on the menu that it needs longer hanging than any other game to ensure tenderness, even without a suspicion of highness; that when underdone it is very unpleasant, and that it responds particularly well to being very quickly browned in fat or in a very hot oven and then cooked in greaseproof paper with a nut of butter and a spoonful of water.

Balkan Cold Meat

Sharpen your knives, for this must be cut thinner than the best-cut ham. It is a fine summer dish. Dispose the meat on ice-cold plates, and garnish each with at least six kinds of pickle or chopped salad, with due regard to colour. On the most thunderous evening, meat served like this can be eaten by people who could have sworn it was impossible to swallow anything.

Tomato Dumpling

Cut large, firm tomatoes in two. Scoop out the centre, mix the pulp with very thick cheese sauce, fill the halves with it, tie them together with white cotton, and egg and breadcrumb them twice over. Put them in a covered self-basting dish, with a spoonful of butter, unless you have a deep pan of boiling oil available—and cook for twenty minutes in a moderate oven.

Cheese Marrow Fritters

These are a delicious luncheon dish, especially in hot weather. Slice the marrow and leave it to drain in a colander under a sprinkling of salt for an hour. Then dip it in pancake batter flavoured with grated cheese, and fry it in very hot fat. Sprinkle the fritters with cheese and brown them under the flame.

Pineapple Fruit Cream

This is an excellent way of using up those left-overs of fruit which complicate the day after a tennis party or dinner. There are a few raspberries, or a few strawberries and cherries, and three or four plums, perhaps.

Drain some tinned slices or chunks of pineapple, and tease them out with a fork into their smallest flakes. Put the whole strawberries or raspberries and the stoned cherries or plums with these, and pour over them a cream or beaten-egg sauce. Chill it without icing it, and it will not taste at all like a left-over.

The pineapple syrup will do excellently for a fruit salad next day, or will greatly brighten stewed apples, if used instead of water. If fresh pineapple is available serve the mixture in the scooped-out fruit, with its tuft of leaves as a lid.

12

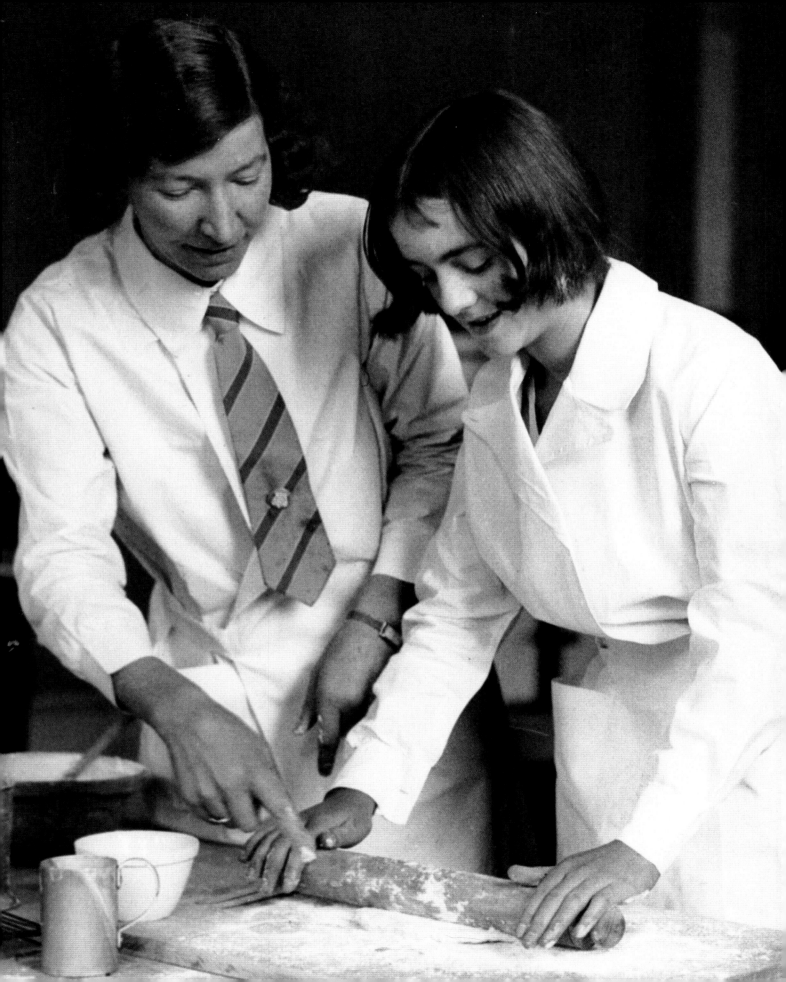

HINTS FOR AMATEUR COOKS

by

DORIS B. SHERIDAN

SECRETS *of* SUCCESS

WHEN making a layer cake trim the edges with a very sharp knife before icing, so that the cake has a perfectly smooth appearance.

"COMMON sense and a good cookery book. That's all you need," said the bridegroom-to-be to Sheila, his fiancée, a typical modern girl with a B.A. degree and a responsible office job.

"That's all very well," put in the fourth member of the party —mathematics mistress at a well-known girls' school, who has taught herself her cookery in the bachelor-woman's flat which is her greatest pride.

"Admitted you need the common sense and the cookery book, but what about the simple things that the cookery books take for granted?"

Practical Tips From Experience

She produced from her handbag a small cookery book—a little gift for Sheila—and, turning its pages, she continued: "Here is a simple example of what I mean.

"In this recipe for macaroni soup half an ounce of macaroni is required, and you are told to add it boiled and rinsed and cut into small rings.

"How can one expect a novice like Sheila to know that macaroni and its fellows spaghetti and vermicelli must go into boiling salted water for anything up to twenty minutes?"

She continued her criticisms through the various sections of the book and we talked cookery for the rest of the evening.

Almost daily in my Bureau work I come up against this lack of basic instruction in recipes.

"Why is my short pastry hard?" is a question which I have answered privately to several readers this week.

Had their recipes told them to use merely sufficient cold water to make the mixture hold together instead of saying vaguely "mix with cold water," this difficulty need not have arisen.

"Why do the cherries always sink to the bottom of my cakes?" is another of the popular queries of the moment. The fruit should be washed in warm water to remove its stickiness before it is dried, floured, and added to the mixture. It is inevitable that sticky or moist fruit should disport itself at the bottom of a cake.

The Way To Grill

Grilling seems to cause a certain amount of heartbreak among several readers.

Whether the grill should be hot or cold when the food is placed beneath it is a surprisingly frequent question. As a rule a cookery book will tell you to "place under a red-hot grill," but few will explain that all grills of fish or meat should have oil poured over them (melted butter will do, if you prefer it); that fish should be sprinkled with flour before it is put beneath the grill; and that seasoning must be added after cooking. To season before grilling merely results in wet patches on the surface of the food that will not readily brown.

To-day's Economy Recipes

BEETROOT SOUP

MELT an ounce of bacon fat in a large saucepan, add one large sliced beetroot, three cut-up tomatoes, a chopped onion, a cut-up carrot, and a small piece of cut-up turnip. Cook together for ten minutes over a slow fire and add a quart of stock and half a pound of haricot beans, which have been soaked overnight.

Season with salt and pepper and simmer all gently for two hours. Pass the soup through a sieve, return to the saucepan with a teaspoonful of vinegar, and re-heat.
. . . .

MOCK CHERRY PIE

THIS is Thanksgiving Day, so here is a cranberry recipe from America. Mix together half a pint of cranberries cut in halves, a teacupful of seedless raisins, a tablespoonful of flour, and two tablespoonfuls of sugar. Place this in a pastry-lined pie tin, dot over with flecks of butter, cover with a top crust, and bake very thoroughly so that the under crust is well cooked. Try this—the menfolk all enjoy it.

SOMETHING HOT FOR SUPPER, *Please!*

By Jennifer Snow

THOSE chilly, unfriendly week-end suppers with their cold joint and quivering blancmange! No wonder husbands want to boss the home to the extent of demanding firmly something *hot* for supper.

Naturally, the woman who has to cope with the Saturday or Sunday supper single-handed wants labour-saving dishes. But if there is no hot-pot, curry, or shepherd's pie ready to heat up, she

need not resort to the cold remains of the luncheon beef.

Here are some recipes for which the ingredients are likely to be in the larder.

Cheese Pudding

Grate some cheese until you have enough to fill a pint measure, then grate breadcrumbs on the same grater—so that you get the full value of cheese—to make an equal quantity. Grease a fireproof dish, make a layer of breadcrumbs, then one of cheese, and sprinkle with salt and pepper, adding a little made mustard and a suspicion of cayenne.

Continue the layers, finishing with

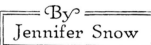

The Eternal Question

There's porridge and bacon for breakfast,
Eggs and a cup of tea,
But what shall we have for luncheon?
That's what is puzzling me.
Tea? Oh, that's perfectly simple,
Cake and a scone or two,
But what shall we have for dinner?
What can I give them new?
I know why I'm getting wrinkles,
I know why my hair turns grey,
It's just this eternal question,
What shall we have to-day?
D. A. G.

breadcrumbs. Beat two eggs, add to half a pint of milk, pour it over, put dabs of butter on top, and bake for about half an hour.

Cheese Spaghetti

This can be prepared beforehand. Cook your spaghetti in quickly boiling salted water until tender, then drain away the water and add plenty of grated cheese, a good-sized piece of butter, a dash of various piquant sauces, and good seasonings. Heat, stirring occasionally, and make quite sure you have plenty of cheese in the dish.

With Tomato

Use the same ingredients, but make in a fireproof dish with layers of spaghetti and cheese. Heat half a pint of tomato pulp with half a pint of beef stock, adding a clove of garlic and seasonings. Cook for five minutes, then remove the garlic, pour the stock over the spaghetti, and bake in a moderate oven for half an hour.

Savoury Meat

Take the gravy left from lunch, add some tomato sauce or any other piquant sauce, and heat in it slices of cold meat. Flavour with a minced pickled walnut, and when very hot pour on to a dish which has a rampart of mashed potato. Or, if preferred, the meat can be served on a bed of hot boiled macaroni.

Baked Eggs and Rice

Grease a baking dish and put at the bottom half a pint of cooked rice mixed with half a pint of tomato sauce. Break six eggs carefully on to the rice and sprinkle with a gill each of grated cheese and grated breadcrumbs, mixed together. Add dabs of butter and bake in a hot oven for ten minutes.

PICNICS AHEAD!

By Helen Simpson

HOT weather—let us hope—and a holiday!! Immediately we pack our picnic baskets or fill our haversacks, and rush away to the nearest sea, or to the country, where the harvest is in progress and the heather already purple, and have as many of our meals as possible in the open air.

One gets a little tired of sandwiches, even though there are so many different varieties we can make. What about some patties for a change? Veal, ham, and sausage patties, for instance, or lobster. Then there are little Cornish pasties, Scotch eggs, and home-made sausage rolls.

All these things are delicious, and they have one great advantage over sandwiches—they have to be made the day before, and so are all ready to pop into the picnic basket. We all want to avoid that early morning rush of cutting sandwiches to-morrow!

An Easy Recipe

A quarter of a pound of ham, sausage meat, and cooked veal will make ten patties. The ham and veal should be minced, mixed with the sausage and flavoured, and a teaspoonful of chopped parsley added. The mixture should be moistened with a little stock.

Divide the pastry into ten pieces, cut out each piece into a round of about 5in. in diameter, and put a spoonful of the mixture on each. Then moisten the edges with a drop of water, and draw them together, pinching them securely. Turn them over and gently shape them into small buns, making a hole in each and decorating them with little shapes made from the remainder of the pastry. They should be baked in a hot oven, and flaky pastry should be used.

Another kind of veal and ham patty is made with the veal and ham mixture to which are added a teaspoonful of grated cheese, a little grated lemon rind, and a level tablespoonful of flour, moistened with a little cream or stock. In this case the sausage is omitted, and the patty cases are already made and hot before the mixture is put in.

Lobster patties are filled with a mixture of good tinned lobster made by putting an ounce of butter in a saucepan, adding flour (a tablespoonful), mixing it smooth and adding, mixing all the time, a quarter of a pint of milk.

Stir while it boils for a few minutes, add seasoning, take it off the fire, and add the lobster cut into little pieces. Add a teaspoonful of lemon juice, and if liked a tablespoonful of cream. Fill the patty cases with the mixture.

Making the Cases

The patty cases should be made of puff pastry, baked in a moderate oven. When they are ready, take off the patty cover and put the case in the oven for a minute to dry before adding the filling.

Cornish pasties have as their filling thinly sliced raw potatoes, chopped raw onion, and chopped raw meat, well seasoned. Each square of pastry (about six inches in size) should have a layer of potatoes, a layer of meat, and a layer of onion.

The mixture should be put in the centre of the pastry and the edges brought together and moistened with beaten egg. They should be cooked in a hot oven until the edges of the pastry are sealed, and then cooked slowly for about an hour and a half. Cooked meat and vegetables should not be used.

The pastry is made with three-quarters of a pound of flour, a teaspoonful of baking-powder, and five or six ounces of lard or dripping. Mix the flour and baking powder, rub in the lard or dripping and make into a thick paste with a little water. It should be rolled out to the thickness of about a quarter of an inch.

For sausage rolls use flaky pastry, and add half a cooked sausage to each square of it. Pinch the edges together, and brush over with milk. Make two or three holes in each roll, and bake in a hot oven for about twenty minutes.

Lettuce travels well if it is wrapped in grease-proof paper and then in a napkin or cloth. It should, of course, be washed and crisp before being packed. The small round tomatoes travel best, and they should not be over ripe.

A squeeze of lemon juice on the lettuce is excellent. The lemon should be packed whole in the picnic basket, and not in halves or slices. A few cheese biscuits are also a good addition to the meal.

Fruit should be chosen with care. Plums are too soft to pack well. Small juicy apples and pears are best, and if there is room a tin of fruit is good—but don't forget a tin opener.

For Thirsty People

If possible allow a vacuum flask for each person. Tea is really better if the milk is added later, so take one flask of milk and the rest of tea. Just in case the milk runs out, take an extra lemon, and use a slice of that instead. Russian tea is most refreshing. If you are going somewhere where you know that you can get a jug of water, take some lime juice or orange, grapefruit, or lemon squash, and a vacuum flask of ice chips.

Rock cakes, coconut rocks, and rice buns are better than slices of cake, which are so apt to crumble or get dry.

Don't forget the sugar and salt—and bury or take away all litter such as paper bags, tins, paper plates and cups, and ice-cream wrappers.

Make rock buns for to-morrow's picnic—they carry so well. Note the special wire rack for cooling cakes fitted to the stove in the picture.

Meals at a Moment's Notice

Tinned fruit, cleverly used, makes decorative trifles.

AN emergency meal is not difficult to contrive from a well-stocked store cupboard, if we remember that instead of simply using things just as they come out of their tins, we should combine tinned and fresh foods to make appetising dishes.

Take soups, for instance. Nearly all "ready-made" vegetable soups are made extra good by using milk instead of water; and to improve them still further, try adding a spoonful of cream to tomato, celery, or pea soup just before it comes to table. This is not so extravagant as it sounds in these days when so many people possess the small machines for making cream from butter and milk.

Instead of serving corned beef in a cold lump, try shredding it coarsely, and mixing with chopped cold cooked potatoes, a little onion and an egg, and frying in dripping. Served with poached eggs on top and a sprig or two of parsley, this will seem quite a recherché dish.

Tinned peas can be made to taste like the fresh vegetable if heated in a colander, with a good-sized lump of butter, over a saucepan of boiling water. Asparagus can be used in omelettes, or for dainty tea rolls, and carrots from a tin heated with butter or a little cream will make a useful vegetable dish.

Try mixing tinned and fresh fruit for a fruit salad.

Tinned fruit make excellent trifles, using the juice to moisten sponge cakes, placed in individual dishes, and spreading the fruit on top before adding the custard. Use a few of the berries for decoration.

SPAGHETTI
is No Joke!

SPAGHETTI has been slandered too long. Most people think of it in one or both of the following ways:—

1. As the cheapest thing on the menu.

2. As a joke, the good old joke of a fat man trying to eat it without getting wound up in the coils.

"Oh, it will make you fat," protest the slimming enthusiasts. Probably they have never seen a thin Italian, but there are really a great many—and they all eat it!

Not Mere Starch

Properly treated, it is a complete food. Of course, you must eat lots of butter with it, and grated cheese and a good sauce of tomato and onion and whatever else you happen to have in the house. So it can no longer be called "just solid starch."

It is nourishing, but you mustn't eat bread with it, or potatoes, if you want to keep your girlish figure. But eaten instead of other starches it fills their place and more.

There are those who can go right on to a fillet steak afterwards, but for ordinary appetites a green salad will be enough. I need hardly add that a good red wine makes the meal not only better but celestial.

The reason, I have come to believe, why this great food is so badly treated in England is that few people, unless they have been to Italy, have ever really tasted it. And even if they have been to Italy they probably avoided it as something gross and excessively difficult.

People will serve it on toast, improving neither the toast nor the spaghetti, which should never be served with any other starch.

Don't Wait

Spaghetti is not difficult to cook, but it must be done properly. And it must not wait after it is cooked, or it will go soft and mushy. That is why, in most restaurants—even Italian ones—there is nothing to recommend it beyond the price. It must be cooked separately for each order.

First, you must have a really big pot, the bigger the better. There ought to be at least three quarts of water to a pound of spaghetti, and it should be well salted and boiling really violently before the spaghetti goes in.

It will take about twenty minutes to cook, and in the meantime you are making the sauce, or sugo, the smell of which no appetite can resist.

With Garlic

Start with some olive oil in a saucepan. When hot add chopped onion, parsley, and garlic (unless you absolutely can't stand it—just a little, and you won't regret it, I assure you). Now add tomatoes, or tomato paste, or both. Fresh tomatoes are good, but I really think tinned ones make a better sugo; use lots and let them simmer down a long way.

Salt and pepper, and it's ready; but it will be much improved by the addition of meat stock or essence, or chopped ham, or chicken or chicken livers, or mushrooms, or a little bacon, all finely minced. Taste and see. The sauce really decides the flavour, and can be varied infinitely

"It takes about twenty minutes, and in the meantime you are making the sauce."

at the discretion of the cook.

The spaghetti itself needs tasting, too. Never trust the clock. It must boil violently all the time, and is done when it is still quite firm but is not starchy in the middle. You can tell best by rubbing a piece between your fingers.

Pour it into a colander and drain thoroughly, shaking it so as to get all the water out.

Then serve. It saves time, heat, and trouble, and is consequently better, to serve directly into individual plates; soup plates are easiest when it comes to the eating. Let several lumps of butter melt into each dish; add the sauce on top, and there you are.

Grated cheese, of course, follows to taste. Parmesan cheese is best, but rather difficult to obtain unless you have an Italian store nearby. Gruyère

"Turn the fork away from you, and go ahead. . . . Bravado is needed."

comes next. Do not use a strong cheese; it destroys the flavour.

Of course, macaroni cheese is very good with cheddar, but in that case leave out the sugo and brown the whole thing in the oven in a fireproof dish. And the French eat boiled macaroni with meat, like potatoes, with meat gravy. It is nice with just butter and cheese, or butter and anchovies and cheese, or butter and capers and cheese; but macaroni sugo is the classic dish, and I think the best.

As to eating it, that takes practice. Turn the spaghetti round your fork, away from you, against the edge of the soup plate, and go ahead. Don't worry about the ends. Bravado is what is needed, and I never said spaghetti was a dainty dish, anyway—I only said it's a good one. BETTY LANE.

"You mustn't eat bread with it, or potatoes."

PUT SUMMER ON The... MENU

Give the children plenty of oranges. A big orange cut in half, depipped, cut into sections, sugared, topped with a cherry, and served like grapefruit, is a pleasant addition to the breakfast or dinner menu.

Mix fruit and vegetables in your salads. Apple, chicory, and walnut is an unusual mixture that will be much appreciated.

THE sudden arrival of warmer weather should be reflected immediately upon the week's menus. This is immensely important not only from the gastronomic point of view but for the health of the household. Weather changes, even for the better, mean a certain lowering of vitality, and if on a warm day one is faced with a meal of the stew-and-suet-pudding type one is either disinclined to eat or, having eaten, disinclined for effort and generally "off colour."

The mere substitution of cold meat and plain salad for the usual entrée is not enough. It needs a good deal of thought to get the planning of the household meals out of the cold-weather routine.

Light Yet Nourishing

When arranging meals for warm weather choose food that is nourishing but at the same time light. It is a mistake to omit all nourishing foods, because the languor supposed to be due to unexpected heat is often in reality partly caused by hunger.

The lighter kinds of fish, such as sole, whiting and plaice, should be chosen: well-flavoured shrimp or anchovy patties are good, and, instead of chops and steaks, try sweetbreads (they can now be had quite inexpensively), veal, brains, and, if possible, a little chicken. Small luncheon chickens at 1s. 6d. are good value, and can be served with "trimmings" to make them go further. Here are some useful recipes for hot weather menus:

Veal Cutlets

Have the veal cut very very thin, then pound it thoroughly. Parboil, then cut into round pieces, sprinkle with salt and pepper, dip in egg and breadcrumbs, and fry in deep fat. Drain well, and serve with a fried egg on top of

By Jennifer Snow

each, crossed by narrow strips of anchovy.

Savoury Sweetbreads

Parboil the sweetbreads, and cut into slices. Take a covered dish, and in it put a thinly sliced onion, two chopped chives, a bayleaf, two cloves, salt, pepper and the juice of a lemon, and let the sweetbreads soak in this for three hours.

Then coat the slices of sweetbread in a thin batter, fry a golden brown and serve with fried parsley.

Brains With Piquante Sauce

Scald the brains in boiling water, then cook for half an hour with two slices of chopped ham, a small beetroot sliced, a small chopped onion, a bayleaf, some parsley, salt, pepper, and a gill and a half of stock (or half a gill of white wine, if you have it, and a gill of stock). Serve covered with piquante sauce.

Fried Brains and Spinach

Parboil the brains, and cut into even-sized pieces. Roll these in beaten egg and breadcrumbs, and fry a light brown in deep fat. Drain well. Serve on croûtons of fried bread, with a border of spinach.

Salads, provided they are cleverly varied, can be served at every lunch and dinner. Sometimes they can be arranged on individual plates after the meat course, or substituted for soup. If you have soup on the menu, make an appetising salad as a one-dish course, with any cold meat or fish you have on hand. Cut the meat or fish into convenient pieces, and mix with lettuce, endive, chicory and watercress, plus a good dressing. Put as many ingredients into the salad as you can, and you will find that a little meat goes a long way, and everyone will enjoy the dish.

Apples with Chicory and Walnuts

A good salad for these days is apple, chicory, and walnut. Take a few crisp lettuce leaves, wash them and shake them dry in a salad basket, and arrange in a bowl or on individual plates. Wash the chicory, and chop into dice. Peel the apples (Worcesters are crisp, juicy, and excellent for salads). Arrange the chicory and apples in layers on the lettuce, cover with dressing and garnish with a few peeled and chopped walnuts.

Sweets should be light and above

all appetising. After a salad meal, a sweet omelette is delicious and nourishing. Or try the lightest of cheese soufflés instead. Now that eggs are cheap, soufflés are a reasonable luxury for any menu. Make your jellies with milk instead of water, and serve such things as junkets (coffee, caramel, or chocolate) and fools made with custard and fruit purée.

Whipped Rice

Rice pudding is more appetising if cooked carefully in the ordinary way and when cool removed from the skin and whipped up with a little cream and the beaten white of an egg. Heap in a deep dish and sprinkle with flaked chocolate (drinking chocolate sold in flaked form can be used for this).

If fresh fruit has not already appeared in the salad, serve it at the end of the meal. A good-sized pineapple can now be had for 1s. 6d.

English housewives to-day realise what an ultimate economy it is to invest in a refrigerator. Food is kept crisp and cool, there is no danger of contamination of any sort—provided the inside of the box is kept scrupulously clean—and the provision of iced drinks and sweets is possible at all times with its help.

Pastel Coloured Refrigerators

I have just seen a new and very attractive-looking refrigerator of the ordinary ice-box type. This is 30in. high and 36in. long, and, having a white porcelain top, takes the place of the ordinary kitchen table. It has 5½ cubic feet of storage space, and, with its primrose-painted "bodywork," is a decorative addition to the kitchen equipment.

This refrigerator-table costs £10 18s., but there is a smaller box-refrigerator, also prettily painted in a range of pastel colours, that can be had for £3 18s. For households where there is electricity, there is, of course, a big choice of mechanical refrigerators, a new "baby" model being priced at £19 10s.

TO-DAY'S French Recipe

OMELETTE MARIETTE

Ingredients

SIX eggs, three medium-sized boiled potatoes, three tomatoes, peeled and freed from seeds (the tinned variety will do), four ounces of butter, and pinch of salt and pepper.

Method

Beat up three eggs on one plate and three on another. Cut potatoes and tomatoes into thin slices and fry in half of the butter, stirring with a fork until partly mashed. Put aside in a warm place.

Now heat a fireproof dish in the oven and put in the remainder of the butter. When hot, add three well-beaten eggs. When these are partly set, spread the vegetables over them and cover with remaining three beaten eggs. Bake in a hot oven until golden brown. This will be sufficient for four people.

The RAMBLER'S FOOD and DRINK

by Claude Fisher

FOOD and drink can make or mar the Whitsun ramble, cycle tour, or camp, as indeed they can any outing, even for the least fastidious of us.

So, whether we elect to cook our feast, or whether we take it with us, it is worth a deal of care.

A favourite method of mine when rambling or cycling is to buy from where I happen to be some fruit, biscuits, and some unsweetened chocolate. For a light meal these are excellent, and a call later for a lager or a cup of tea or other drink completes a welcome repast.

Our British lack of imagination in the sandwich line, more particularly among private individuals, is amazing. Ham, beef, or hard-boiled egg form many ramblers' sole resources, and frequently super-dry and uninviting at that.

ALLURING SANDWICHES

Yes, I am criticising. I feel entitled to after tasting such alluring sandwich fillings as mayonnaise-covered salmon and lobster on anchovy paste; bananas and honey amid brown bread or scones; and pounded and shelled walnuts with cream cheese.

So I counsel you make your sandwiches with imagination. Try toast instead of bread for a change. It is satisfying. A toast sandwich evenly spread with butter to which chopped parsley may be added and with small sardines lying side by side, seasoned to taste, is a meal in itself.

Biscuits, too, such as cream crackers, digestive biscuits, and the like, make tasty and varied sandwiches. So do scones. And here are some more fillings. Gruyère and all the cheeses, especially cream cheese,

which can often form the basis for other ingredients such as chopped gherkins, almonds, salted or plain, sliced apples, red currant jelly, all of which, however, make tasty enough sandwiches on their own. Hard-boiled yolk of egg mixed with creamed celery or shredded onion and sardine are others.

TOOTHSOME MORSELS

Sponge fingers with sweet fillings are toothsome morsels. Try strawberry jam and cream with them, or a fruit mixture.

Here is a jolly one: 1lb. prunes stewed with sugar, ¼ gill of cream, ¼lb. almonds and vanilla essence beaten together.

If you must have ham or beef or their kind, salad—green or Russian—sauces of all kinds, pickles and chutneys make good companions.

But there are other solid and not very imaginative fillings; sausages of all kinds, pork and beef, liver, breakfast and luncheon; smoked salmon;

chicken, game, pork, brawn, rabbit, tongue.

The tea-maker in camp or by the wayside will find it worth while carrying a small muslin bag or a square of muslin in which to place the tea and insert it in the pot. Allow for the leaves to swell.

Of other drinks—and the thermos type of flask keeping them hot or cold, as when starting, is a tempting proposition—coffee and chocolate will occur to all.

What about mocha for a change, half coffee, half chocolate, or one of the meat extracts?

Lemonade, orangeade, grape fruit, and limejuice cordial are common enough cold liquids. But have you tried a cider or claret cup or some other cup? Pineapple lemonade is uncommon but good. Half a pint of water and ½lb. sugar boiled to a syrup with a couple of lemons and a small tin of pineapple grated up will, when diluted, make a pint and a half. But get all the new milk you can when in the country!

He who cooks may read, but he will never cook decently until he practises. No writing can teach him, only guide him.

SMALL FIRES BEST

Let him learn then without unnecessary experiment that the cooking fire should be small and manageable. The ideal is a heap of white hot ashes laid where a turf has been removed and placed aside to replace when finished. For safety sake lay the fire away from overhanging branches, bushes, bracken, stacks, and the like.

Some campers fry eggs on flat stones, but most of us prefer pots. A frypan and two or three nestling pots with handles are necessary for comfortable provision for, say, three campers.

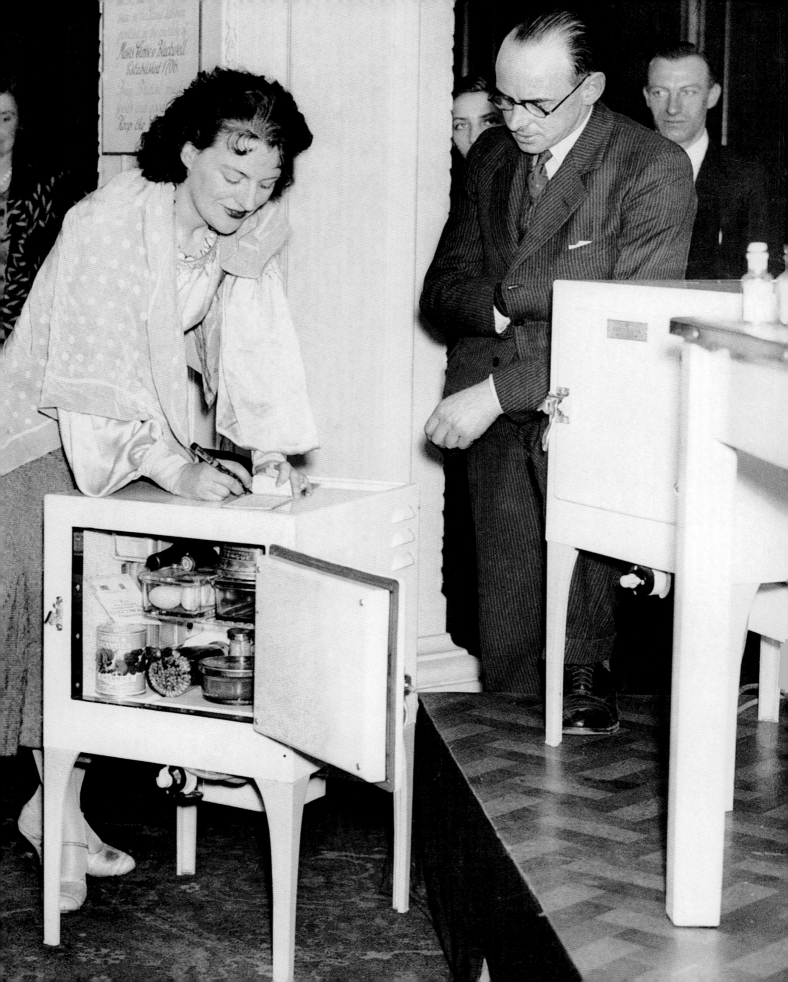

Are You Tired of Salads?

—Then Try Some of these New Ones

By Countess Morphy

INSTEAD of the usual salad-bowl mixture, Countess Morphy suggests a novel way of stuffing cucumbers.

SCENE — any British home. Time — any mid-August evening of 1933. Dinner is being served : there is the usual salad-bowl on the table. Says any husband, " My dear, I'm tired of this rabbit-food." Says any wife, " Well, what else can I have this hot weather ? And salads are so good for you, darling."

Of course we're all bored with " rabbit-food " after a whole summer of heat-wave, when salads seem the only possible fare. But salads needn't be just " rabbit-food," by any means. Try something rather special in this line and there will be no more complaints of the monotony of the plain lettuce-tomato-cucumber alliance.

Apples for a Change

Apples are cheap and plentiful just now and are very refreshing in hot weather. An attractive salad can be contrived by making a neat round incision on the top of an apple, then removing the core without piercing the other side of the apple, removing a little of the pulp, and filling the cavity with fresh gooseberries. Garnish with a few shredded almonds, previously blanched.

Prawns in Cucumber

Cucumber need not be " plain sliced." What about choosing a firm and straight cucumber and cutting it in 2½ to 3 inch lengths? Remove the seeds and some of the cucumber pulp, and fill with chopped prawns that have been mixed with chopped lettuce, seasoned with a little salt and moistened with a little oil. The same can be done with beetroot, choosing the larger kind, and stuffing with some of the beetroot pulp, chopped lettuce and cucumber.

An ordinary beetroot salad is greatly improved by the addition of grated horseradish and a few caraway seeds. The white part of an uncooked cabbage, finely shredded and mixed with dessert apples, peeled, cored, and thinly sliced, also makes a delicious summer salad.

And now that melons are cheap and plentiful, all manner of delicious fruit salads can be made with them. They are very refreshing stuffed with either raspberries or gooseberries, or sliced and mixed with plums or grapes.

All these salads are at their best served very cold. When ice is available they should be put on to it an hour or so before serving.

Cooking at Table

NOT only the bachelor girl in her flatlet, but also the housewife who has to cater for a family of five or six, will appreciate these useful electric gadgets for cooking at table—particularly during the rush hour between rising and racing for the morning train.

The electric toaster and coffee percolator are already too well known to need mention, but one of the

latest breakfast appliances is a gadget which makes toast and coffee simultaneously. The bread is put into a little tray under the percolator and the same heating element serves both purposes.

Another useful table-cooker, containing three small compartments, will make toast, poach eggs, and grill bacon. Although it is quite small and light enough to be lifted with one hand, it is capable of keeping pace with half a dozen healthy appetites.

Then there are various kinds of table cookers which contain a small oven. These are miniature replicas of the standard family cooker, and are intended chiefly for use in the small flat. They can provide a three-course dinner for two or three persons, and are usually installed on a small " dumb waiter " and wheeled to the table when required.
M. E.

CHRISTMAS COOKERY

is EASIER NOW!

By Doris B. Sheridan

GETTING ready for Christmas! To the women of past generations this meant hours of kitchen industry, the careful picking over of fruit, the accurate measurement of ingredients, the boiling of puddings, and the baking of cakes.

The old order has changed in so many ways that, wondering whether modernity could infringe upon such an old-established custom as the home preparation of Christmas foods, I spent yesterday visiting the provision departments of several of London's largest stores. On all sides I heard stories of orders for Christmas fare already placed, of demands for cooked puddings and hams, decorated cakes, mincemeat packed in its jars, and—already—for mince pies.

The modern woman has a diversity of outside interests, and at home she is confronted with the problems of small flats and their accordingly minute kitchen accommodation. Who, therefore, can blame her if she goes the shortest way about achieving an end which took her mother, even with excellent domestic assistance, many hours of thought and hard work ? A reliable store, supplying goods of first-class quality ingredients, can, at little extra cost, solve her problems for her. Is it to be wondered that she is taking advantage of these up-to-date labour-saving devices ?

* * *

AT the same time old customs die hard, and there must be thousands of women cheerfully and pleasurably undertaking the task of preparing all the Christmas fare at home. It is, as in all these matters, a question for personal choice.

The pudding, for instance. You can buy it ready in its cloth-covered basin, requiring only the hour or two of final boiling inevitable before any

self-respecting Christmas pudding is ready to appear on the dinner-table. Or you can do the job yourself from start to finish, again making use of a tried and tested recipe.

If this is your decision do not forget that the blended mixture will improve if it is set aside in a cool place under a clean cloth for twelve hours before it is divided among its buttered moulds or basins, and that at least eight hours' steady boiling or nine hours' steaming will be required for the first cooking.

* * *

MINCEMEAT you can acquire in jars all ready for use in such quantities as you will need. If you make your own supplies, remember that the frying of the chopped apple in a little butter improves the general flavour, and, above all, observe the necessity for the air-tight jar.

The actual pies you will, of course, make as you need them. Whatever type of pastry you embark upon, be sparing of the water. Too much water is responsible for many pastry failures. While we are on the subject of pastry, I saw an interesting novelty at one of the stores which would be useful for the Christmas week-end. For a few pence you can buy a nicely browned cooked pastry crust, complete even to the sprinkle of caster sugar, and packed in greaseproof paper in a carton. With it you can purchase a tin of fruit, and, if you do not already possess one, a standard size piedish to fit the crust. All you have to do is to pour the fruit into the piedish, fit the crust on top, and put the complete

ORDERING Christmas cakes and puddings well in advance—a typical snapshot taken at a London store where a 50lb. Empire pudding is displayed.

pie into the oven for fifteen minutes. Result—fruit pie that will satisfy the needs of four people.

* * *

NOW we come to the all-important Christmas cake. Here again I heard of tons of cakes, iced, adorned with seasonable decorations, and ready for the table, being ordered. Even so, I think the home-made Christmas cake is in a class by itself, and that its vogue will not so readily be relinquished.

From my correspondence I gather that one of the chief difficulties experienced by readers in the making of these large, rich cakes is that of fruit sinkage. This is caused by too moist a mixture, the use of fruit that is not absolutely dry, or by incorrect oven temperature. Cakes with a large proportion of fruit should be put into a hot oven at first to "set" the fruit, after which the heat should be reduced to enable the cake to cook slowly and thoroughly.

It is quite a good plan to stand the tin containing the Christmas cake in a second and larger tin filled with a mixture of salt and sand, as this will prevent the cake from acquiring that too-hard brown crust sometimes resulting from the necessary long period of cooking.

* * *

THE "half-home-made" Christmas cake is another sign of the times. Some people will buy the cake and ice it them-

selves ; others will make the cake and buy the type of prepared icing that requires only to be mixed smooth in cold water before it is spread over the cake. If you make your own icing, remember that hard beating and a little lemon juice produce the white glistening finish which characterises really well-made royal icing.

Then there are the decorations. I saw iced plaques with seasonable greetings; Father Christmas figures with or without the appropriate reindeers and sleighs; robins on tree stumps or pillar boxes; Eskimo children; snow cottages and many other ready-made decorations which obviate any need for proficiency with the icing-bag and pipe.

* * *

GINGER wine, that time-honoured Christmas beverage, is still made by many of my readers. For those who wish to buy their supplies in advance there is a wide choice of wines packed in effective containers of china or glass that could do service as decanters or vases when the Christmas festivities are over.

This "eye to future use" was also apparent in the containers in which some of this season's preserved ginger is packed.

Another good "buy" for Christmas is the cocktail set comprising three bottles in a neat case, one containing salted almonds, a second olives, a third cherries, and the whole rounded up with a bunch of cocktail sticks.

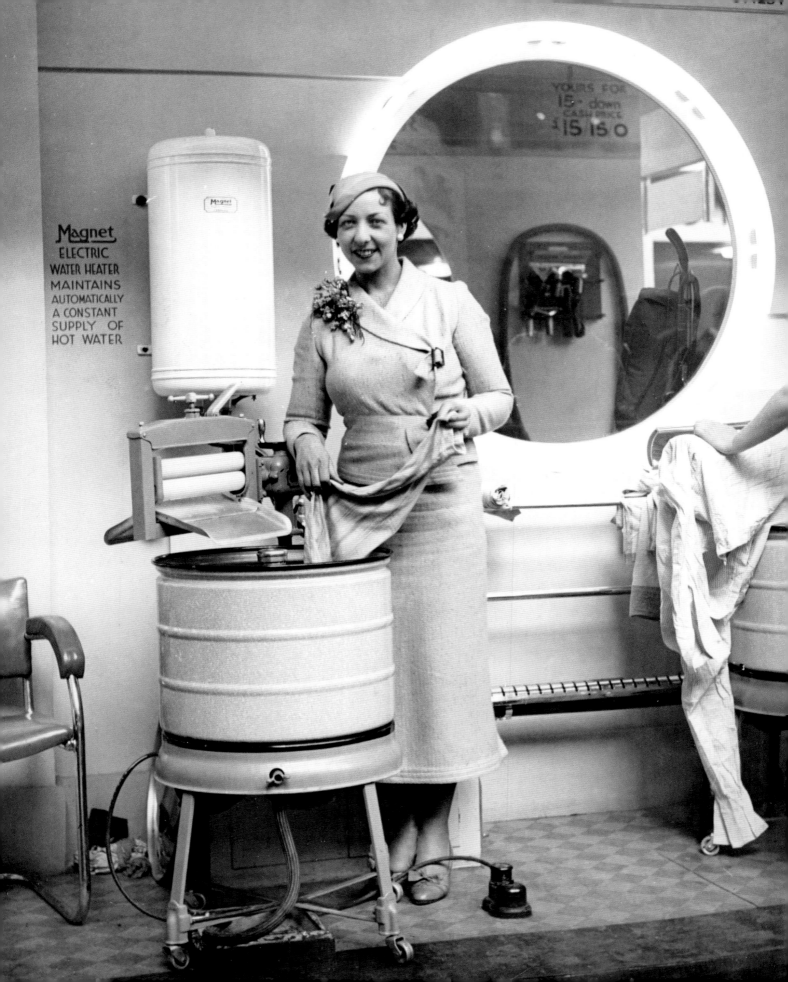

Household Hints

Imagine - no servants! These are make-do-and-mend suggestions for middle-class wives making the best of life without housemaid or cook. A dirty raincoat? Rub it with hot salt. Stained wallpaper? Use a little French chalk sprinkled on bread. Discoloured linen? Soak it in buttermilk, rinse in water and spread out on the lawn to dry. Preservation and economy are the watchwords: this is not a throwaway society. Beetroot keeps if you add a little mustard to the vinegar; leftover parsnips can be made into cakes and served with bacon for breakfast. Onions can be stopped from sprouting if the root end is held briefly over a flame. Much of this lore is still valid: windows rubbed over with a paraffin rag will repel the flies; sour milk cleans gilt frames; small rooms are made larger by painting skirting boards the same colour as the carpet. Hints that lamp wicks can be made from old felt, and tapers can be made by melting candle ends in a saucer and drawing bits of string through the wax, remind us that electric light was not universal. Apples are as much a staple as potatoes: made into fritters with bacon for breakfast, cooked with brown gravy or stewed into an apple souffle. The luxury item is the refrigerator, newly accessible on a middle class income. It needs to be rinsed inside with a good scouring agent, washed and dried. For households which cannot aspire to a fridge advice is given on how to build a meat-safe.

ANTIQUE FURNITURE, after the polish has been applied on a soft rag, should be rubbed up with a fairly stiff brush, used, of course, in the direction of the grain. This brings up the full effect of the markings on the wood. The same method should be used on oak floors.

* * *

BEETROOT FRITTERS make a welcome addition to the menu. Stew some beetroot until tender, cut into slices, dip in egg and breadcrumbs, and fry. Serve with white sauce and hard-boiled egg passed through the sieve.

* * *

BRASS BEDSTEADS and handles which have become shabby can be made to look like new by painting them over with a special gold paint. This lacquer will last for years without tarnishing. Any rough surface should be removed with sandpaper.

* * *

CANDIED PEEL that has become hard through storing can be softened and made easy to cut if it is placed in a hot oven before use.

* * *

GOLF JACKETS of suède or leather are apt to tear on the shoulder from the friction of the bag strap. Buy some strong adhesive tape, now obtainable in many colours, to match as nearly as possible, and stick the tear together on the inside. If this is done neatly so that the torn edges just meet it will be almost unnoticeable.

* * *

HAM will be found delicious, and rather like the celebrated Virginia variety, if when boiling it you use cider instead of water. If necessary add a little water and place one medium-sized apple, stuck with a few cloves, in the liquid.

* * *

LIVER will not be tough if you fill a small soup plate with new milk, dip each slice of liver into this so that it is completely covered, and lift out and place at once in boiling fat without draining.

* * *

MATTRESSES can be kept from rusting if a little floor polish is applied to the metal parts with a brush.

* * *

MILDEW STAINS can often be removed by moistening soft soap and starch with the juice of a lemon. Spread the paste over the mildew, lay out, and bleach. Afterwards wash in usual way.

* * *

ORANGE SLICES may be used instead of apple sauce as an accompaniment for roast pork. Cut the fruit into thin slices, soak for half an hour in lemon juice, a little sugar, salt and pepper, and place on the pork chops or round the joint. Garnish with parsley.

* * *

SOUR MILK makes a good cleaner for gilt picture frames. Simply rub with the sour milk and dry with a clean duster. This will not remove the gilt, as other methods often do.

* * *

TOMATOES, if unripe when picked, should be placed at once in a drawer and kept in complete darkness for a few days. This will quickly ripen them off, while retaining their freshness.

* * *

VACUUM FLASKS should not be corked when stored after use. Rub the cork all over with common salt to prevent a musty flavour, washing it well before using the flask. If this is done no paper cover will be needed.

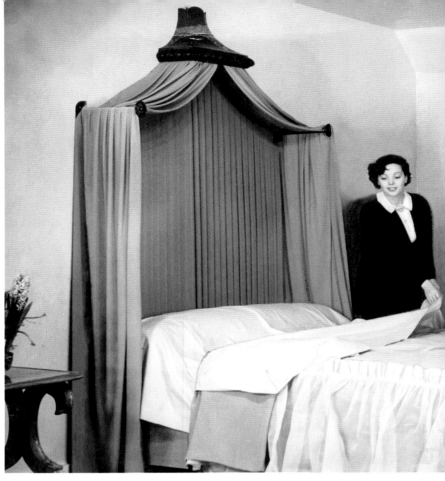

HOUSEHOLD HINTS A B C

LINGERIE SILK should be washed in a solution of lukewarm water and pure soap flakes. Squeeze the garments, rinse out thoroughly in several changes of water, wring lightly by hand, and hang over a line to dry. Do not peg out, and when ironing do so on the wrong side with a cool iron. A hot iron will render the silk fibres brittle, and should never b used.

* * *

MAITRE D'HOTEL BUTTER, such a useful accompaniment to steamed or boiled fish, is very simple to make, although it sounds complicated. Mix together with the point of a knife equal quantities of butter and freshly picked chopped parsley, gradually adding a few drops of lemon juice and seasoning with salt and pepper. Keep in a cool place until required. This is quick to make and can save the making of a sauce if in a hurry.

* * *

PLANTS grown in pots should always be watered in winter with water of the same temperature as the room or glasshouse in which they are kept. Stand a can of water in a warm place ready for use.

* * *

SILK STOCKINGS which have been washed should, when nearly dry, be rubbed with a flannel till all moisture is extracted, when they will not require mangling or ironing.

* * *

VEGETABLES left over may be used for Russian salad. Cut the cooked, cold vegetables into dice and spread in a shallow bowl. Add some salad dressing, decorate with strips of beetroot, tomato, or celery, and finish with anchovy.

The Latest Slimming Exercise Is—
HOUSEWORK!

Sweeping and Dusting Your Way to Beauty

[Fanny Inglis.

Does your housework make you slim and supple? It would if you did it in the right way. Compare these pictures—then learn how to get slender while you do your daily dusting. This is an ideal beauty regime for busy women, who can thus turn the most trivial household task into a slimming exercise.

On the extreme left is shown the right way to dust beneath low furniture, using a long-handled mop. The wrong way to sweep is demonstrated in the next picture.

"I HAVE so much housework to do that there is no time left for slimming exercises," sigh hundreds of busy women.

But actually the very tasks of which they complain can, if done rhythmically and with the correct poise of the body, maintain just that slimness and grace which every woman desires.

Housework exercises are now taught by a London school where women learn rhythm in everyday tasks. Of course, it is essential that each movement should be done in the correct way, otherwise there will be round shoulders, hollow backs, and a general lack of poise.

Even Strokes

The second figure above shows such a common attitude adopted for sweeping that at a glance there appears little wrong with it. But the woman is straining forward, head poking, back hollowed, with her weight thrown heavily on one foot.

Instead, she should be standing almost upright, changing her weight from one foot to the other as she sweeps, moving her broom evenly over the floor in time with a rhythm which she hums as she works. The broom touches the floor at the beginning of each stroke on the beat of the tune, and is never raised far above the floor or stretched out far enough to interfere with the poise of the body.

The right way to polish floors is important. There is usually a strain, lack of balance, hollow back and bent left arm in the wrong attitude.

In the correct position the weight is rested on the left arm so that the right is free to polish the patch in front without undue stretching and without moving the kneeling pad. Again, every movement, even the single twist necessary to put polish on the cloth, is done to rhythm.

How do you mop under low-built furniture? Do you go down on both knees, drop your head almost to floor level, and push the mop vigorously to and fro? Or do you stoop until your back nearly breaks, and you hate these new, low pieces?

Forward—Lunge!

On the left is the way to do it. Remember the "forward-lunge!" of your school gymnasium days. This is the same exercise. With the weight on the forward foot, and back and right arm straight, make circular movements until the dust is brought well forward and then fetch it out with short, straight strokes.

And through it all the breathing must be deep, regular, and through the nose, so that no dust is inhaled through the mouth.

When you wash up, don't lean over too far, or, by way of contrast, stand heavily on your heels and push out your diaphragm. Stand easily on the balls of the feet and keep the diaphragm in and the head well poised. Change the pace of the tune you hum according to the state of your crockery, for greasy dishes require slower, more thorough washing. Always wash plates with circular movements *away* from you.

Household Hints ABC
For Your Own Domestic Dictionary

ALMOND MERINGUES are an original party sweet. Make an ordinary meringue mixture, but add to every two whites of eggs 2oz. of ground almonds, folding this very lightly in just before cooking.

• • • • •

BEEF TEA CUSTARD is a nourishing dish for invalids and small children, and makes a welcome change from ordinary beef tea. Slightly whisk two eggs and gradually add a teacupful of good beef tea, stirring well all the time and adding a little salt and pepper to taste. Turn into small buttered moulds, cover with greased paper, and steam until set. Let the custards stand for a minute or two before turning out, otherwise they are liable to break.

• • • • •

COAL FIRES with ugly tiled surrounds may be transformed with a little sheet brass or copper. The brass is cut to the right shape and "sprung" into the sides, and another piece is made to cover the floor-tiles. The total cost of one such renovation amounted to 6s.

• • • • •

FIG SANDWICHES are a popular item for a picnic lunch or tea. Mince some dessert figs with half their quantity of seedless raisins, add some finely chopped blanched almonds, and mix in a good sprinkling of lemon juice. This filling is best with wholemeal bread and butter.

• • • • •

GREASE on coat collars may be removed easily if eucalyptus oil is applied. Rub gently with a soft rag.

• • • • •

IRONS, especially if they have been used for garments that have been starched, should be cleaned before they are put away. Wash them in hot soapy water, to which a teaspoonful of ammonia has been added.

If no starch has been used, the usual rubbing on wire gauze is sufficient to clean the iron.

• • • • •

LACE CURTAINS will last longer if they are placed in a pillow slip before putting them in the copper. This obviates the risk of tearing them when using the copper stick.

• • • • •

ORANGE TEA makes a delicious summer drink when it is iced. Allow half an orange and one teaspoonful of tea to each person. Squeeze the oranges, add ¼ pint of boiling water, bring to the boil again, and infuse the tea. Fill up with boiling water, stand for five minutes, and pour off. Allow to get perfectly cold, and serve with a small lump of ice in each glass.

PIQUE frocks should be ironed on the wrong side to bring up the pattern. Remember to use a slightly cooler iron for linen than for cotton, as it scorches more easily. And when washing out voile frocks ready for the summer, put a little vinegar in the rinsing water and use a very little starch to make the material crisp.

• • • • •

RICE balls for schoolroom puddings can be made in this unusual way. Cook 3½oz. of rice in one pint of milk until tender. Add 1oz. of sugar and chocolate flavouring or vanilla essence. When cold form into balls, dip in beaten egg, toss in breadcrumbs, and fry. Sugar, and serve with custard or chocolate sauce.

• • • • •

STOCK, provided it is strong, can be made into a filling for sandwiches if a little gelatine is added. Then allow the liquid to cool, and it will set into a jelly. Season to taste.

ALMOND LEMONADE makes a change from the ordinary kind, and is an extremely refreshing summer drink. Boil in a quart of water the thinly pared yellow part of the rind of two lemons, the juice squeezed from them, 2oz. of ground sweet almonds, an ounce of bitter almonds, and ½lb. of loaf sugar.

Simmer for about ½hr., then strain and allow to get cold. It can be served with soda water added, if liked.

* * *

BROOMS AND BRUSHES will not mark the furniture and paintwork if a piece of rubber beading is fixed at the ends above the bristles. Nails with rounded heads should be used, as they will not cut the rubber.

* * *

CARBON PAPERS can be made to last twice as long if the inked side is held before a fire until the surface looks new again. Creases can also be removed if the paper is carefully stretched while it is held before a fire.

EGG SAUCEPANS may be easily cleaned by putting two dessert-spoonfuls of ordinary salt into the pan and rubbing well with a stiff brush. Rinse with hot water.

* * *

FINGER PLATES cut from mirrors are quite as attractive and more practical than those made of glass. As the latter are transparent, it is not always easy to see where they are, while the former not only reflect the fingers, but catch odd lights in the room in a way which makes them very decorative.

* * *

GLASSWARE of the ornamental type will have added lustre if it is polished with a clean duster that has been soaked in paraffin and then dried. This will also discourage flies.

* * *

LAMP WICK can be made, in an emergency, from felt. Cut an old hat into strips of the width required.

MELONS that have been cut into before they are ripe need not be wasted.

Cut some slices about an inch thick, pare off the rind and lay in a shallow glass fireproof dish. Lightly sprinkle with soft sugar, and cover with water to which has been added, and well stirred in, a tablespoonful of black currant jam. Cover the dish and cook in a slow oven, turning the slices occasionally, until the liquid is reduced and the melon nearly clear, like cooked marrow.

This can be eaten hot or cold. Beaten white of egg could be used to top the dish if liked.

* * *

SAFETY RAZOR BLADES which have been used are a useful addition to the work basket. They are invaluable for unpicking machine stitched seams.

Keep them in a specially marked box to avoid the danger of cutting fingers. A slotted metal holder can be obtained to take them.

SMALL ROOMS can be made to appear larger by painting the skirting boards the exact shade of the carpet. This increases the apparent floor space.

The photograph shows a room with honey-yellow walls, green hangings and a black carpet, with a black skirting-board to match. Note the little recess where objets d'art are displayed upon glass shelves, and also the plain wooden pelmet painted the same colour as the walls.

NOW is the time to make a Simnel cake for Mothering Sunday. First make almond paste by mixing together in a bowl 1 large egg, 6oz. of ground almonds, ¼lb. of caster sugar, and a squeeze of lemon juice. After well pounding together, divide this into two portions, flatten one out on a plate to a round the size of your cake-tin, and keep the other for decorating the top of the cake after it is cooked.

The cake mixture is 8oz. self-raising flour, 6oz. caster sugar, pinch of salt, 6oz. butter, 10oz. currants, 4oz. candied peel, 3 eggs.

Cream together the butter and sugar, gradually add the eggs, which have previously been well whisked, then stir in lightly the flour and pinch of salt, the cleaned and dried currants, and the peel chopped small.

INTO a cake-tin lined with two or three thicknesses of greased paper put half this mixture, then a layer of almond paste, and cover with the other half of the cake mixture. Press it down a little towards the centre so that the cake does not rise in a peak. Cover with grease-proof paper to prevent the top from burning.

PUT into a hot oven, and when the cake has risen, lower the heat and bake slowly for about 2 hours, until a fine skewer or knitting needle comes out clean when pierced through the centre.

Put a band of almond paste round the outer edge of the top of the cake, mark it with a fork, and make little balls of almond paste to put inside this rim. Brush the almond paste with a little beaten egg and return to the oven until it is set and slightly browned. Turn on to a wire sieve to cool.

A row of cotton-wool chicks and a fancy paper band similarly decorated will give the cake its traditional appearance. This also makes a splendid birthday cake.

ANCHOVIES may be used to make an inexpensive substitute for caviare. Take about six, wash and bone them, and pound them with pepper and salt, a little dried parsley, lemon juice, and touch them with a fresh clove of garlic. Make into a paste with olive oil, and serve on dry biscuits.

BANANAS may be baked in the oven in their skins. Cut off the ends first. When the skins burst take them out, peel them, and serve with sugar, cream, and a sprinkling of lemon.

CANDLES that do not fit the holders need not be shaved with a knife. Dip the bases into boiling water, and they will be found to fit any candlestick.

CORNER CUPBOARDS for the kitchen are obtainable in unstained wood for 37s. 6d. They are six feet high and are fitted to hold brooms and other kitchen utensils. To paint them to match the kitchen décor, sandpaper lightly and apply stain or washable paint.

FISH cooked in a casserole with onions and ham makes a savoury dish. Put into a casserole ½pt. of milk, a little water, one finely chopped onion, a tablespoonful of chopped ham, 1oz. of margarine, and some pepper, and simmer for ten minutes.

Wash and cut up 1lb. smoked fillets of fish, and simmer in the liquid for half an hour. Thicken the liquid with flour and serve with the fish and mashed potatoes or toast.

LINEN may be speedily marked through a copper plate in which the name has been cut in any one of a large variety of types. To brush over the plate, leaving a perfect impression, takes only two or three seconds.

MACKINTOSHES in which a clean rent has been made can be repaired with the adhesive tape used for medical purposes. Carefully shear the edges of the tear, place closely together, put a piece of tape over the join at the back, and press gently with a warm iron.

MATCHES of the non-safety type should always be made stored in a tin box, especially if the house is being left for any period. If mice get into the cupboard where the matches are and gnaw at the box there is a risk of its catching fire.

NEWSPAPER AND MAGAZINE TIDIES, made of cretonne or any strong material toning with the furnishing scheme of a room, are extremely useful for holding magazines and papers which are still in use by the members of the household. They are made like an open bag, the width of a chair back, the two top hems being run through with wooden rods to keep the bag stretched taut.

The under-rod is tied at each end to the back of a chair near the top.

ONIONS should be served frequently in cold weather, to prevent colds. Skin and parboil several Spanish onions, take out the centres, and stuff with minced meat, well seasoned.

APPLES that are heavy and, when pressed between finger and thumb, give a slight crack, are the best for all culinary purposes.

BLOTS and smudges on letters, as well as ink, fruit, tea, coffee, and ironmould stains on white and fast-dyed fabrics, may be tackled with this handy pencil, which can be carried in the handbag.

It contains a stain-removing preparation, a drop being applied to the spot from each end of the gadget.

* * *

CHEESE dishes will be more digestible if a pinch of bicarbonate of soda is added during the cooking.

ELECTRIC LIGHT CORDS in the kitchen and wherever the atmosphere becomes hot and steamy should be covered with rubber tubing. It is easily put on, and costs very little. Rubbing with a soapy rag twice a month will keep it clean.

* * *

GLASS TOPS for dressing-tables or chests of drawers can be contrived by buying inexpensive bevelled glass shelves and " packing " them as panels over lace or silk linings. They will give an individual smartness and are labour-saving.

* * *

ICED TEA with vanilla ice cream is a refreshing summer drink. The tea should be made rather stronger than for drinking hot in the usual way. When it has stood for seven minutes pour it from the leaves, sweeten it to taste, and stand in the refrigerator for some hours. Serve in dainty glasses with a spoonful of vanilla ice cream on top of each.

IRONING at home will be easy if you remember that *linen* irons best when *quite damp, cotton and muslin* when somewhat dry, and *artificial silks* practically dry.

Stockings and flannel pyjamas should always be ironed on the wrong side, as well as all heavy embroideries.

* * *

MARROWS are cheap now. To pickle them, take two or three small marrows, 1 quart malt vinegar, one nutmeg (grated), 1 oz. grated horseradish, 1 oz. salt, pinch of cayenne. Peel the marrows, slice in half and remove all the pips. Cut into fine dice. Boil for five minutes in well-salted water.

Drain, and place the vegetable in a preserving pan with the vinegar and other ingredients. Boil again for five minutes. Pack the marrows into the jars, pour the liquid over them after straining, and tie down at once.

PUTTY can be made for domestic repairing purposes by mixing linseed oil with whitening until it is of a workable, doughy consistency.

* * *

RED TILED FLOORS will have a deeper and richer colour if a little paraffin is added to the water with which they are washed.

* * *

SILVER LACE on uniforms and fancy dresses can be cleaned and brightened by applying powdered magnesia with a brush. Allow to settle for two hours and brush off with a clean brush dipped in spirits of wine.

* * *

WILD FLOWERS usually wilt immediately if they are picked in the ordinary way and placed in cold water. But if the stems are put in boiling water as soon as they are picked this will seal them, so that the flowers will last some time. A little salt in the water helps to keep them.

Spring cleaning is the time for renovations. Here are some new furnishing ideas.

SIMPLICITY of line and an absence of projecting angles are features of the furniture illustrated, which has been designed to take the place of built-in fitments in the small flat. The sideboard above, of English walnut, has been made rather low to accommodate rows of bookshelves above and around it. The low occasional table is also of English walnut.

ANTI-SPLASH nozzles attached to water-taps should be fixed so that the flow of water is directed into the waste pipe. In this way splashing is reduced to a minimum and an efficient flush provided for the waste pipe.

* * *

BATHROOM MATS of crêpe rubber sometimes become hard and curl up at the edges in cold weather. This can be remedied by immersing the mats in warm water until they become soft again.

* * *

BOLSTER CASES on the American pattern are easy to make at home. The under-piece of the case is made the length of the bolster with about 6in. folded in at each end. The top part is made with an overhanging piece. This can be finished with hemstitching or embroidery, and looks well hanging down at each side when the bed is made.

* * *

CRACKLING is more likely to be crisp and brittle if it is rubbed with lemon-juice before the pork is cooked. An additional flavour is given if the crackling is very heavily scored and finely chopped onion, mixed with powdered sage and good seasonings, is rubbed into the interstices before the joint is put into the oven.

FRYING without fat is a good method with chops and steaks. Sprinkle a thin layer of salt in the pan and let it get very hot before cooking the meat for a minute on each side. Afterwards fry slowly for four or five minutes on each side.

* * *

INK STAINS on the fingers can be removed by brushing with a soft nail brush dipped in pure vinegar, and then in salt. The same stains on material should be washed in vinegar and then rinsed well.

THE tiny dressing-table, of English cherrywood, shown on the left, can also be used as a writing desk. Placed at right angles to the window, it avoids blocking up the light. The sheepskin rug costs 35s.

LINEN should never be stored in a cupboard near a hot-water cistern or other source of heat. In a warm, dry atmosphere it is liable to become dry and brittle, and even to turn yellow. Choose a cool, fresh place, free from damp, to preserve its whiteness and silky sheen and prevent mildew or discoloration. Linen to be stored for any length of time should not be starched in the final laundering.

* * *

MILDEW ON CLOTHES may be removed in a variety of ways. Rub in damp salt and leave the garment in strong sunshine if possible. Repeat next day if necessary. Or soak the

ROUNDED edges and a top covered with black cowhide are features of the walnut writing desk above. The drawer fronts are of cherrywood with rosewood handles, to tone with the chair of honey-coloured cherrywood covered with a rose-coloured silk rep.

stain in sour milk for several hours and then put it into the sunshine without rinsing. Lemon juice may remove slight stains.

* * *

PICKLED CABBAGE will remain crisp if a small piece of washing soda the size of a nut is added with the spice to the vinegar.

* * *

TULIPS and other flowers with fleshy stalks are often inclined to droop and flag when first put into water. If they are left lying horizontally in cold water overnight the stalks will stiffen wonderfully, and they will remain firm and upright for some time.

Another way is to wrap each head in newspaper from within an inch or two of the end of the stem, and leave standing in a vase all night.

* * *

WASTE-PAPER BASKETS of the wicker-work variety can be painted to match the colour scheme of the room. Wash thoroughly in soap and warm water, and allow to dry perfectly before painting. Use any reliable brand of cellulose paint. Basket chairs may be treated in the same way.

PERMANGANATE of potash or iodine stains can be entirely removed from cotton and woollen materials by rubbing immediately with a cut lemon.

• • • • • •

RUBBER HOT WATER BOTTLES will last much longer if they are washed out once a month with warm water to which a little soda has been added. This should be done whether they are in use or not.

The rubber will keep pliable and will not perish if treated in this manner.

• • • • • •

SATIN SHOES may be successfully recoloured with the liquid dye sold in bottles and intended for straw hats.

Before dyeing, stuff the shoes tightly with crumpled newspaper. Do not

• • • • • •

WINE which is being decanted should have a lighted candle or electric bulb placed just behind the neck of the bottle. This makes it possible to see the first sign of sediment. Stop pouring before this gets into the decanter.

• • • • • •

WOOLLEN COATS and jumpers dry more evenly and keep in better shape if a cane is passed through the sleeves instead of the usual coat hanger. Suspend the cane from the clothes line.

RICE for milk puddings requires about six times its weight in milk. If this point is remembered there is less likelihood of puddings being too dry. Always wash rice in a sieve in plenty of cold water.

* * *

STAINS on the skirting board and the lower parts of furniture are a frequent occurrence when the amateur tackles floor staining during spring-cleaning operations. Keep a bottle of turpentine beside you when doing the job. A quick wipe with a rag dipped in this will immediately remove the stains.

Household Hints ABC

For Quick Reference in Domestic Difficulties

For cold day lunches, vary that well-known dish, "Surprise Potatoes."

APRICOTS (dried) make unusual hot sandwiches. After soaking and cooking till soft, put through the mincer, sweeten, and stew until pulpy. Use as sandwich filling when cold, scattering the bread with powdered cinnamon. Toast the sandwiches on both sides and serve hot.

*   *   *

BATH TOWELS that are wearing thin in the centre can be utilised to make hair shampoo towels. Fold the towel in half, end to end, and cut a slit up the centre of one half as far as the fold. Then cut a circle, about fifteen inches in diameter, out of the middle of the towel, at the top of the slit.
Bind the edges with tape, thread a draw-string through the circular part, and wear over the shoulders when shampooing the hair.

*   *   *

CASSEROLES that have been cracked —this may happen if the dish is placed, while hot, on a cold surface—

can be repaired for kitchen use. Clean the casserole with a brush and hot water in which a little soda has been dissolved. Mix thinly a small amount of the best cement, obtainable from any builder or the building department of most stores, and let this run into the crack.
Leave the casserole for a few days to allow the cement to set thoroughly. Afterwards, it can be washed and used again.

*   *   *

CROUTONS to be served with soup are made by toasting bread and cutting it into dice about half an inch square, which are then fried in deep fat. After being taken out of the fat they should be put to drain in a warm oven or in front of the fire for a few minutes.

*   *   *

DINNER WAGONS with a highly polished surface sometimes become badly marked by hot dishes. To prevent this, procure some coloured felt, which can be bought in 36in. widths, cut to the size of the shelves and fit in. Choose a colour to harmonise with the dining-room. The decorative effect can be enhanced by appliquéing small circles of coloured felt to each corner

*   *   *

FISH CAKES are best when "bound" with a good purée of potatoes, consisting of mashed potatoes moistened with milk and butter to form a paste, in which the flaked fish is blended. Paint the cakes with beaten egg, dip in breadcrumbs or vermicelli, and fry very quickly in deep boiling fat from which a faint blue haze is rising.

*   *   *

MARKING-INK STAINS on white linen should be treated as soon as possible after they have been made.

First soak the marked part of the fabric for a moment in a solution of one pint of water and a half-teaspoonful of permanganate of potash. This will reduce the stain to a brown mark.
Rinse well in cold water and then soak the fabric in a weak solution of peroxide of hydrogen, rinsing this out when the stain has disappeared.

*   *   *

POTATOES can be made into very tasty little lunch or supper dishes if cooked with eggs as a variation of Surprise Potatoes. Choose large, even-shaped potatoes, and bake them in

their jackets. Cut off a piece at the base to make them stand up, scoop out some of the pulp, drop in a little tomato ketchup and seasonings, then, very carefully, an egg.
Add a dab of butter and a little more ketchup, bake long enough to set the egg and serve with chopped parsley.
Potatoes in the half-shell are cooked in the same way, except that they are cut in half, and all the pulp removed, well mixed with the egg, and seasoned before being returned to the shell.

For spring refurbishing—a delightful new suite in light oak, designed for a small flat, lends itself to a leaf-green and brown colour scheme for a bedroom. Complete with a roomy wardrobe, 5ft. 10in. high and 3ft. wide. Note the attractively shaped frameless mirror.

TO HELP THE CHRISTMAS PREPARATIONS

ALMONDS for the Christmas table need not always be salted. Try soaking them for two minutes in boiling water; then, without blanching, place them on a tray in the oven, and grill them until the skin will rub off easily. Send to table hot in little bonbon dishes without removing the skins.

. . . .

BALLOONS for Christmas decoration will blow up more easily and are not so likely to burst if they are first put near the fire to warm slightly and well rubbed between the palms of the hands.

. . . .

CHESTNUTS are cheap just now. Try making chestnut cream for a party sweet. Roast about 30 nuts, taking care not to discolour them, peel and skin them, and pound in a mortar. Add enough milk to make a paste, put in an aluminium saucepan, beat together a pint of milk, a knob of butter, 4oz. of caster sugar, and the yolks of two eggs, and boil all together for 5 to 10 minutes. Strain and cool off.

. . . . .

DUCK OR GOOSE can be made more interesting by using this mixture to stuff it. Cut up the livers and boil with a large onion until tender. Drain off liquid and keep it. Mix the rest with six large chopped apples, half a pint of

breadcrumbs, a gill of stoned raisins, and seasonings, and use with enough of the liquid to moisten.

. . . . .

ECONOMY COCKTAILS can be made without the usual ingredients and still give a festive air to parties. Use equal quantities of lemon or orange squash (the sort that is usually drunk with ordinary or soda water) and French and Italian vermouth, and shake together. Add a little soda water

CHRISTMAS AT HOME

will be all that you could desire if you watch the "Daily Mail" women's page.
You will find dozens of helpful menus and suggestions for catering and cooking, besides original ideas for entertaining guests of all ages. There will also be useful dress and beauty hints for the holiday.
Read this page every day.

to each glass when it is poured out, and finish with a cherry or a piece of lemon or orange peel.

. . . . . .

HOLLY LEAVES can be frosted for garnishing purposes by first washing well in clear water and wiping with a cloth. Then spread on a flat dish in

a warm (but not hot) place until thoroughly dry. Dip each leaf first into lard that has been melted until it is liquid, and then into caster sugar. Dry well in a warm place and store in tins until required for use. These leaves are not, of course, intended for eating.

. . . . . .

ORANGE SALAD is made more attractive if it is decorated with marmalade jelly dotted round the border of the dish in which it is served.

. . . . . .

PLUM PUDDING SAUCE can be made in this way. Put into a jar 1oz. of caster sugar, the yolk and half the white of an egg, and half a wineglassful of brandy. Stand the jar in boiling water and beat up the contents for 10 minutes.

. . . . . .

YULETIDE CAKES to represent snow scenes are effective and are much quicker to ice than the more elaborate varieties. Instead of putting on the icing smoothly, make it as rough as possible, and when almost set give it the effect of snow by shaking dry caster sugar over it. Finish with a little Christmas figure.
A band of decorated paper, sold for the purpose, gives a Christmas air and saves spending time on the sides of the cake, which are always more trouble than the top.

Suspended from a shelf of blue enamel and stainless steel are (left to right) an apple corer, tin-opener, potato and vegetable masher, potato and fruit peeler, knife sharpener, and cutter for garnishing and shredding. The set costs 7s. 11d.

Below this is an aluminium container with adaptable name disc, 1s., and a collapsible sandwich box, 3s. 3d.

NUT BUTTER is a delicious filling for sandwiches. To make it, shell and blanch any nuts, and grind them to powder before mixing with butter. The mixture should be pounded until it is of a perfectly smooth consistency.

* * *

OVEN CLOTHS which will prevent the hands being burnt by hot pans and meat tins can easily be made. Take a double strip, 30in. long and 12in. wide, of a strong material such as hessian or coloured crash. Sew these two strips firmly together, then sew an additional piece, 10in wide and 4in. deep, at either end, stitching round three sides so that they form two pockets into which the hands can be slipped when removing hot tins from the oven.

* * *

PASTRY will keep crisp for a longer period if it is mixed with milk instead of with water.

* * *

RAZOR BLADES which are too blunt to be used in the ordinary way have many domestic uses, if they are of the perforated type. They can be nailed across loose joins of wood on screens and furniture, choosing an under or back part which is out of sight. This repair is strong and neat.

* * *

REFRIGERATORS need careful cleaning. Remove the shelves and wash these and the inside of the refrigerator with a good scouring agent. Rinse with hot water and wipe perfectly dry. Wash the frame with warm, soapy water, rinse with clean water, wipe, and leave the door open until the whole is quite dry. Any felt or baize may be washed occasionally with warm soapy water, using a soft nailbrush.

STOCKINGS should be darned diagonally, not in the direction of the weave. They will then "give" more easily and so wear longer. A large hole in the leg of a child's stocking should first be filled in with open net, and patched diagonally, before darning through it.

* * *

SUET will keep well for some days if it is skinned and chopped very finely and then completely covered with flour to exclude air.

* * *

TILED HEARTHS should not be washed if this method tends to split the enamel and glaze. Take a cloth dipped in turpentine and rub them till they are clean. Finally rub with a dry cloth.

* * *

TINS which have become rusty can be restored to their original brightness by rubbing them with a rag dipped in sweet oil and whitening, afterwards cleaning and polishing in the ordinary way.

* * *

VEGETABLES should never be left in the stock-pot or they will spoil its contents. Peeled and sliced vegetables can be added to the pot before it is boiled, but after the stock has been poured off they should be carefully removed from the bones, which can be used again.

* * *

WALLPAPER that has become soiled by dust or smoke can be cleaned by rubbing it over with a flannel dipped in oatmeal.

ARTIFICIAL FLOWERS which look bedraggled will be improved if the edges of flowers and leaves are trimmed with a sharp pair of scissors. Then shake over a steaming kettle and allow to dry in a draught.

BAKED MILK PUDDINGS, such as sago or semolina, are much nicer if sprinkled with grated sponge cake and coconut—a thin layer of each. It will brown beautifully, and has a delicious toasted flavour.

BLACK SHOE POLISH that is too dry for use should be moistened with a little vinegar. In a household where a great deal of polish is used, it will be found to go farther if slightly diluted with vinegar.

* * *

CARPET SWEEPER brushes should be regularly cleaned by means of a wire brush. Every thread and hair should be carefully removed by this means before putting away the sweeper after use.

INKSTAINS on silver can be removed by rubbing the stain with a mixture of whitening and sweet oil made into a thin paste. Leave this on for a day, afterwards washing and drying. Finally polish in the usual way.

* * *

LINEN which has become slightly discoloured should be soaked in buttermilk for one or two days. Rinse first in cold and then in warm water, and spread out on the lawn to dry.

APPLE SOUFFLE is a light and appetising sweet with which to conclude a hot meal, and can be cooked in the oven while the other dishes are baking. Stew in the oven in a casserole some thinly sliced apples with water, a lump of butter, sugar, and grated lemon rind. Beat to a pulp and mix with the beaten white of an egg, and bake for a few minutes in a greased oven dish.

BEDSPREADS of artificial silk usually have two seams, one on either side. If these seams are covered by a braid about one inch wide, with another length of braid crossing the bedspread at an equal distance from the top and bottom to correspond, a new and fresh appearance can be achieved with very little trouble.

CHENILLE CURTAINS should never be rubbed or squeezed when washed. They should be dipped up and down in a warm, soapy lather made from soap flakes, and left in the water for a few hours. Rinse in warm, slightly soapy water and hang out wet. Press while still damp.

EGG added to soup to make it more nourishing should be beaten first, and the hot soup poured slowly over it. If only the yolk is being used, beat it with a very little milk—then pour the soup over it.

FOWLS that are rather "elderly" can be made as tender as chickens if rubbed with lemon juice, then wrapped in buttered paper. Steam for two or three hours according to size. The fowls may be roasted after being partly steamed.

HOLES in wood which have been caused by nails or screws can be filled up by pressing in a paste made by mixing together fine sawdust and glue. When dry, the surface can be evened by rubbing with sandpaper.

JAM SPONGE ROLLS will not crack in cooking if this method is followed. Remove the sponge from the oven and turn out on a clean, damp cloth. Trim the edges, spread with jam, and roll up quickly.

KNIFE HANDLES that have become stained can usually be cleaned by rubbing with a piece of damp flannel dipped in table salt.

MIMOSA is far less likely to lose its fluffiness if, immediately it is bought, the stems are scraped for an inch or so from the ends and then plunged into boiling water for two minutes. Then put them in water in the usual way. The flowers should thus remain fluffy for several days.

NAILS driven into plastered walls usually become loose as soon as any object, such as a heavy picture, is suspended from them. They can be rendered perfectly safe and firm by this method. Drive the nail into the wall, remove it, and fill the cavity with a mixture of plaster of paris and water. Place the nail in this paste so that it will harden round it.

PANS which have been used for frying fish or onions frequently retain a slight odour. Swill them round with water and vinegar after scouring, and this will disappear.

VARNISHED FLOORS which are to be restained must be thoroughly cleaned before any fresh stain is applied. To remove the old varnish, wet the boards with a solution of strong and hot soda water. Allow it to soak well in, then scrub hard the way of the grain. Rinse with clear, warm water. If any obstinate patches remain rub them with fine sandpaper.

WASHABLE DISTEMPER such as may be purchased dry or ready mixed for use dries quickly and hardens. To obviate this the bucket containing the mixture should be placed in a larger one containing boiling water. The rising steam will keep the distemper smooth and liquid while the walls are being covered. Do not wash the walls until three weeks after the application of the distemper.

Here is a useful stainless knife which will cut grapefruit or oranges into neat portions ready for serving at breakfast or dinner. Its price is 2s.

HOUSEHOLD HINTS ABC

MANY "Daily Mail" readers have already contributed tried home hints to this useful Wednesday feature. Why not send in your labour-saving ideas? The payment for each hint published is Five Shillings. Address your letter or postcard to The Editress, "Daily Mail," Women's Page, Northcliffe House, London, E.C.4.

IF you are "moving house" this month you may have to cope with the problem of the ugly Victorian fireplace. Here you see how the fireplace in an old-fashioned house has been modernised at very little cost.

The fire surround, which includes a marble mantelpiece, has simply been boxed in with plywood and fitted with an up-to-date fire. A fitment of this kind could be made by any joiner. The colour scheme is grey, green, and silver, a modern washable wallpaper in light pastel green being used for the background, the fireplace itself being painted a soft grey. The "steps" at each side of the recess are faced with silvered metal, which reflects the light of the fire and gives a warm, glowing effect.

AMMONIA should be added to the soapy water in which washleather gloves are washed. A few drops are all that will be necessary, and will keep the gloves perfectly soft.

*   *   *

BACON for boiling will have a better flavour if a dessertspoonful of vinegar is added to the water.

*   *   *

CARPETS or mats can be prevented from curling by applying some very thick starch on the edges. Place a piece of brown paper over the starch and iron dry with a fairly hot iron.

*   *   *

COOKING SALT will crush more easily if the block is allowed to stand on cold tiles, or on a stone sill, for half an hour beforehand.

*   *   *

FIREPLACES of unglazed red bricks which have become darkened by smoke can be cleaned by scrubbing with undiluted vinegar, using an old nail brush, or similar brush, for the purpose.

*   *   *

HORSERADISH SAUCE, added to scrambled egg or spread on the toast on which poached eggs are placed, give an excellent flavour. Warm the sauce before using.

*   *   *

HOUSEHOLD LINEN can be quickly mended by machine. Fill the shuttle with a medium darning cotton and thread the needle with No. 40 or 50 cotton. Machine to and fro over the hole until it is filled in, keeping the needle down and raising the foot at the end of each row.

*   *   *

INSOLES for shoes, so frequently needed for children, can be cut in an emergency from an old felt hat.

*   *   *

IVORY KNIFE handles will be freed from stains if they are rubbed with a rag or leather dipped in warm soapy water, with a sprinkling of pumice-stone powder. Polish finally with a clean cloth.

*   *   *

LEMONS will keep for a very long time if they are put into a basin of cold water. Be sure to change the water every day.

*   *   *

MERINGUE can be prevented from falling in if enough cream of tartar to cover a sixpence is added to the half-beaten eggs. Continue to beat until firm and bake in the usual way.

*   *   *

ONIONS will not sprout when stored if the root end is held for a few moments over a flame or singed with a hot iron.

*   *   *

PASTRY left over from making tarts, pies, and so on, can be utilised for making delicious little tit-bits. Roll the small pieces out thinly, spread with sugar, and sprinkle with cinnamon. Form into a roll, cut off into short lengths, and bake.

*   *   *

RICE for curries will be dry and flaky if it is boiled as follows. Put a breakfastcupful of rice in a large saucepan with plenty of boiling salted water. The water will cease boiling for a few seconds, but as soon as it again is on the full boil, cook the rice for *exactly* 13 *minutes.*

Pour it at once on a wire sieve, and put it under the cold water tap for a few minutes, stirring it well with a spoon. Drain, and warm up in the oven.

*   *   *

STALE BREAD will be improved if placed in a steamer over boiling water and allowed to steam slowly from fifteen to twenty minutes. The result will be a very light loaf. This is more effective than reheating in the oven.

*   *   *

SUN BLINDS should be cleaned before they are put away. If they are made of glazed cotton they should be rubbed over with bath brick and sponged with a rag soaked in warm, clear water.

If they are really dirty, they should be washed in a good soapy lather, rinsed well, starched, and ironed when damp. Allow to dry before putting away for the winter.

*   *   *

TIES not kept in a tie-press can be kept in order by a simple device. Take pieces of cardboard a little more than a quarter the length of a tie and as wide as its widest part. Double the ties, fold them over this piece of card, and snap two elastic bands round to keep them in place. Two or three ties can be kept on each piece.

*   *   *

VANDYKED GEORGETTE NECK-WEAR, lace edgings, and all fancy-bordered lingerie etceteras will have a professionally laundered finish if you pin them out flat on a clean pillow to dry. Stretch and secure the spiked edges firmly, and when they are quite dry press them lightly with an iron that is barely warm. A hot iron should not be used, as it will press out the crêpe of the georgette.

*   *   *

VEGETABLE MARROW is sometimes overboiled so that the pieces break when strained. If this happens it looks better and tastes excellent if the vegetable is mashed with butter, pepper, and salt. Be careful to drain away as much water as possible before mashing.

FINGER-TIP BEAUTY

WHEN using a nail brush to clean the finger tips, use it also lightly on the cuticle and round the side of the nails. Then brush the hand and wrist to stimulate the circulation and improve the colour of the skin.

Rub hand cream at night from the tips of the fingers down to the wrist, working it in with the same movements as you use to ease on gloves.

Cuticle remover is effective in taking away stains on and under the nails, particularly those made by cigarettes. Apply it with cotton wool, and rub gently.

Rinse the finger tips and dry them thoroughly before applying polish, or it will not give an even appearance. Apply it in long strokes from the base to the tip of the nail.

Manicure polishes and other preparations can be obtained in scents to match one's other perfume.

Fashion

In the late 1920s and early 1930s, fashion responded to the Depression by becoming more sober. Rejecting the glitzy fabrics and decorations of the Flapper decade, women avoided conspicuous display in favour of a new simplicity. Instead of jewelled bangles, leather belts with metal motifs were worn by the young. Studs replaced long earrings. Belted jumpers with plain sleeves were regarded as chic, and glittering jewellery was replaced by simple pearls. Black and white were in vogue - long black high-necked dresses in streamlined satins and silks which were slinky but unflattering to women's curves. In the autumn of 1932, the Daily Mail's fashion editor, Victoria Chappelle, declared "Blouse Jackets are Trumps". To compensate for the severity of the tight-fitted evening wear, gowns were almost backless, a hugely tantalising combination. Another way of relieving the severity was trimming with fur, in the days when every wild animal was fair game for the dressmaker. Monkey fur was much in vogue; so were antelope gloves and ostrich feather boas: they looked good against velvet hats and dresses. Men had their own revolution: not so much the lighter fabrics and louder patterns, in the 'gangster' style of American movies, but new elastic yarns which held up their trousers without needing braces.

WHAT YOU WILL WEAR this AUTUMN

Leading Lines from the Paris Dress Shows. Sketched by ODETTE

Collar of jacket is loose and only 1 inch high. It is cut as part of the front and back. Wide but not "upholstered" shoulders

Jumper buttons at back of neck

A large fur bow and muff is the newest "set"

Short knitted jumper

Cape can be buttoned round waist to form travelling rug when needed

Entire outfit of reversible material, plain one side the other

width on hips

Fur jumper has silk back and upper sleeves

Travelling, sports or informal costume consisting of cloak, skirt, jumper and jacket. The belt has large pocket extensions. It can be worn with or without the jacket

Fur gloves to match sleeve facings

Ecru mosquito net darned with white wool

nearly all collars are loose and high

Very narrow sleeves

slight fulness above waist

Afternoon outfit of black reversible satin. 7 length coat belted and collared in neat new way
Sleeves have bands of shiny side stitched to dull side, of satin white crêpe tunic (¾ length) worn under coat

blouses that can be worn with day or evening skirts.

White chiffon blouse high in front & back with deep slit. Silver fox above elbows. Four crystal bracelets in different shades of one colour.

Black velvet skirt mounted on flesh coloured georgette top for wearing with different blouses coatees, jumper wraps, etc.

46

FASHION *Puts Your* COAT on the Sliding Scale

By
Victoria Chappelle

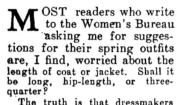

Here is a version of the three-quarter coat, in pearl grey wool crêpe, with coral red striped scarf-collar and trimming, and four buttons placed below the waist.

This snappy sports ensemble is of mouse grey wool, the hip-jacket fastened below the waist with metal clips. Note rolled collar and woollen gloves to match.

MOST readers who write to the Women's Bureau asking me for suggestions for their spring outfits are, I find, worried about the length of coat or jacket. Shall it be long, hip-length, or three-quarter?

The truth is that dressmakers have put coats on a sliding scale this season. There are all the orthodox lengths, including full, three-quarter, and hip-lengths, with a few others which are betwixt and between, such as five-sixths and seven-eighths. The waist-length jacket this year is not prominent, except for the evening. It is improbable that we shall see much of the odd lengths outside the salons, but the first three I have mentioned may be safely taken for granted. The long coat is made on princess lines or belted, the three-quarter coat usually hangs from the shoulders, while the hip-jacket varies considerably.

Fashions *about Town*

THE opening of the London season . . . and a sudden outcrop of the very latest summer fashions in theatres, restaurants and clubs! Here are a few snapshots:

At the theatre—a white piqué dress, accompanied by one of the new collarless, wide-sleeved Eton jackets in garnet-red velveteen. Worn with a posy of piqué flowers. (See sketch.)

* * *

A watch as a bag fastening, protected by a plate of thick crystal which magnified the face and the hands.

* * *

A sailor hat of natural chip straw, which had a square crown rising to a curious blunt point in the centre, and a slightly down-curving brim. Worn with very trim, short hair and set off by pearl-stud earrings, this looked very tailored and chic.

* * *

One of the new ribbon turbans showing the hair at one side. Undoubtedly smart, it was apparently a great trouble to put on. At a matinée the wearer had absent-mindedly removed it and was looking at it in despair. "This means I must spend twenty minutes putting it on again," she said to a friend.

* * *

Several white turbans, with accessories to match, which seems to suggest that white is going to be as fashionable in London as it is in Paris. Short white crochet scarves are much in evidence.

HANDBAGS: *Slim Lines and New Materials at the British Industries Fair*

THE new simplicity in fashion means that great stress is laid on the right accessories. And of these accessories the handbag is one of the most important.

Thousands of new handbag designs are on view at the British Industries Fair. Most of them are severely plain in cut and irreproachable in workmanship and finish. The envelope shape is neglected in favour of the top-opening, which is usually of plain chromium. Sometimes there is a snake-chain of silvered or gilt metal, sometimes the convenient thumb-strap at the back, and sometimes the simplicity of the line is broken by no handle at all.

Below are shown a chromium-frame bag of red patent calf, with black composition ornament, and belt to match; navy calfskin bag with light

BLOUSE JACKETS ARE TRUMPS
this Autumn

By VICTORIA CHAPPELLE

BOTH these evening blouses have the new high necklines in front and deep décolletages at the back, but while the model on the left has the new basque and a cape effect, the other is finished with sash ends which tie below two ornamental buttons. Satin, lamé, or velvet would be suitable materials.

A HIGH neck completed by a bow tied behind the shoulder and a broad belt above the basque are distinctive points on this velvet afternoon blouse.

MOST of us are looking round now to see which of the new fashions will help us to face these early autumn days. It is too early for a coat, and a suit does not altogether fit in with one's still summery mood. The solution of the problem seems to be found in one of the new blouses which, shown in the recent collections, have made a tremendous hit in Paris, and are particularly becoming to the Englishwoman. Made on the jumper principle and worn with a trim skirt, it is responsible for the success of the whole outfit.

ACTUALLY these blouses suggest very light jackets,

and as such must be almost semi-tailored if they are to be effective. Many of them have the new high necks (or can be given one by means of a scarf), which makes them smart for morning.

No flimsy materials are used; velvet is very popular, not only for afternoon but occasionally for morning. The old-fashioned striped velvets, as well as various patterned velvets, may be chosen.

FOR the woman who wants a blouse for practical wear, the most sensible choice, of course, would be a light-weight woollen in a plain or fancy weave. Newer than a deliberate match would be a top in a

lighter shade than the skirt—especially if one of the new blackberry or mulberry colours are chosen—or in a deliberate contrast. The hat, and perhaps the bag, should match the blouse, but the shoes and gloves will look best if they tone with the skirt.

This gives us the opportunity to try out the effect of the new short basque which is fluted only over the hips, leaving the back and the front quite flat. If this does not appeal to you, the blouse can be made to fit over the hips with a plain belt.

❖   ❖   ❖

FOR the afternoon moiré is a good material, and satin has become important again, but although these blouses may have short sleeves and more elaborate necks, they are always on the plain side.

Quite an attractive neck line for a blouse of this type is achieved by simply inserting a couple of broad bands into each side of a fairly low-cut "V"; these are crossed, so that a slight cowl effect is given just beneath the chin, and the ends set into the blouse itself and buttoned together at the back.

❖   ❖   ❖

SHOULDERS are not exaggerated so much this season

—those tremendous frills have vanished—but a slight fullness can be concentrated at the top of the armhole if this suits you. Newer than this, and usually more becoming, is the distribution of fullness between shoulder and elbow in such a manner that it produces a modified pouch, or a series of small ridges or points. But if a plain sleeve is more becoming, do not hesitate to choose it—the collar and, if you want them, some attractive buttons will give you all the elaboration needed.

❖   ❖   ❖

LONDON FASHION SECRETS

Practical Autumn Clothes from English Salons

BY ODETTE

LONDON dress houses are now preparing the collections of autumn and winter models they will show during the next month. From the advance information which I have obtained I can see that British designers will reveal many fresh and fascinating aspects of the new mode, other than those stressed in Paris. This is stimulating news.

Attractive and at the same time practical ideas are dominant in the minds of the London dressmakers.

I note among the leading features of their forthcoming shows :—

Light-coloured cloth or woollen jackets over dark velvet dresses.

Separate capelets, with buttonholes which make use of buttons on the jacket or dress.

Very tailored-looking pinafore skirts that finish at a high waistline at the back.

High, loose collars.

Important but not grotesque sleeves.

Touches of fur on cloth or silk dresses to match the coats worn with them.

The toilettes shown in the sketch give an idea of the originality of line and treatment to be offered by English houses. On the extreme left is a dark brown corded velveteen dress with a white flannel jacket, suitable for early autumn wear.

Next to this is a costume with a high-waisted pinafore skirt in dark and light grey check, a jacket in plain grey cloth with checked sleeves and a separate capelet that fastens at the back and is kept in place in front by five buttonholes which fasten over the buttons of the jacket.

Behind this, one sees a plain black marocain dress, and a back view of the ruby velvet jacket that is worn with it. The next illustration shows the dress of a travelling or everyday costume that is completed by a knee-length cape (not shown).

The seated figure at the extreme right wears a velvet afternoon dress with the loose, high collar that is to be a feature of next season's modes, and rather important looking sleeves in which all bulk is concentrated between a low shoulder line and just below the elbow.

The remaining model is a cloth dress with a touch of fur to match the coat. This coat has a loosely draped collar that hangs away from the neck.

STRANGE FRUITS come to TABLE

ALL SORTS of queer fruits from abroad are now being sold in this country. Many people ignore these unusual things because they do not know how to serve them.

PASSION FRUIT.—The simplest way is to cut off the tops and eat it with a small spoon, rather like an egg. Another way is to scoop out the pulp, mix it with sugar and whipped cream and pile in individual glasses. A few passion fruit added to fruit salad give an unusual piquancy. The juice will make cocktails more intriguing.

CUSTARD APPLES.—Eat the white pulp with a spoon, taking out the large black pips, and adding sugar if liked. Mangoes are eaten with a spoon, too.

AVOCADO PEARS.—For a salad, remove the peel and serve on lettuce with French dressing. Mash the pulp with lemon juice and cayenne for an unusual sandwich filling, or serve as an hors d'œuvre by removing pulp from half shells, mixing until smooth with oil, vinegar, salt, and cayenne, and returning to shells.

POMEGRANATES.—The best way to peel is to cut a small round piece from the top, and then carve down the hard rind in its natural segments, so that the fruit can be pulled apart. A compôte can be made by removing the seeds from some large pomegranates, putting these in a glass bowl and sprinkling with rose water. Make a thick syrup from the juice extracted from one or two more pomegranates with sugar to flavour and an equal quantity of water. Heat until it thickens, let it cool, then pour over the fruit in the bowl. Cape gooseberries can be served in compôte, too.

How I Spend My Dress Allowance

Prizes of Three Guineas, Two Guineas, and One Guinea are offered for the best individual dress budgets by readers. Make an account of your own expenditure, write down in 100 words or less your reasons for making any *one* of the purchases mentioned, and send it to " Dress Budgets," *Daily Mail* Women's Page, Northcliffe House, London, E.C. 4, so that it reaches this office not later than by first post on Monday, November 16. Winning budgets will be published, but only the initials of the senders will be printed. The decision of the Editress must be accepted as final.

FIRST YEAR.			
Winter coat with fur fabric collar	3	19	11
Tweed coat frock to tone	0	19	11
Stockinette jumper suit	1	10	0
Fur felt hat	0	12	11
Sports beret	0	2	6
Proofed gaberdine coat	2	10	0
Evening frock and coatee	2	10	0
Shantung frock	1	9	0
Straw hat	0	10	0
Linen hat	0	5	0
Cotton frocks	1	0	0
Silk washing frock with coatee	1	10	0
Bathing suit and holiday accessories	1	0	0
Stockings	3	0	0
Shoes	3	3	0
Gloves	0	15	0
Handbags	0	15	0
Scarf	0	2	11
Underwear	3	10	0
Odds and ends	0	14	10
	30	0	0

SECOND YEAR.			
Harris tweed coat	2	17	9
Cardigan suit to match	2	2	0
Velvet evening coat	1	10	0
Tweed skirt and pullover	1	0	0
Velour hat	0	10	0
Wool georgette coat and frock	3	0	0
Straw hat to match	0	12	11
Shantung frock and jacket	1	19	0
Shantung hat	0	10	0
Artificial silk frock	0	13	9
Washing silk frock and jacket	1	10	0
Tennis frock	0	10	0
Tennis shoes	0	5	0
Sports coat	0	9	6
Beret	0	3	11
Two pairs shoes	2	2	0
Evening shoes	0	12	11
Stockings	3	0	0
Gloves	0	15	0
Handbags	0	15	0
Underwear	3	19	11
Odds and ends	1	1	4
	30	0	0

JUST over a year ago I was given my own dress allowance for the first time. It is £30 a year. I spent a great deal of time during my lunch hours exploring the shops in town to find out how much clothes cost, and I bought very few at first because I was not sure what would be most suitable for business and "grown-up" life in general.

I have had time to decide what kind of clothes I need and like most, and I have planned out my complete budget for two years. The second supplements the clothes I have left over from the year before. My winter coat is still quite good, for I bought one with a fur fabric collar so that the material should be the best possible for the price.

I shall buy a good tweed coat, and as soon as the sun shines early in the year I shall buy a spring outfit, and my winter tweed suit will be cleaned and worn by itself. After watching how other girls dress I have decided that the most important thing is to match up one's clothes perfectly, so I try to buy a coat and frock at the same time.

Cotton frocks seem to be of little use except for tennis and holidays, for I do not like to see them in an office. So I buy sleeveless silk frocks with a little coat to match, and then I can wear them on almost any occasion. I am very careful to buy only materials which will wash well.

Made in light-weight tweed gaberdine, this 19s. 11d. frock is ideal for office or house wear. The wide revers soften its otherwise severely trim cut, and a lingerie front can be inserted. Buttons decorate the pleated skirt.

One of the prizes of the bargain hunter with a small dress allowance is this evening gown and jacket for £2 10s. It is made in apple green georgette over a silk slip, and the fashionable elbow sleeves of the jacket are trimmed with black fur. The line is simple, the neck being round, and the skirt, which fits closely at the hips, fully flared.

CLINGING HATS—of Elastic!

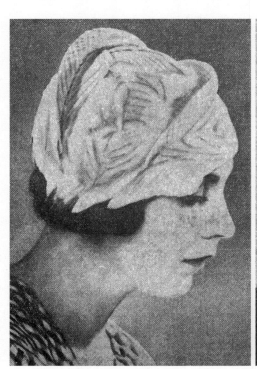

LUXURIOUS curls and the newest hats are not friends, by any means, unless the curls can be arranged to stay outside the hat instead of being tucked within. So consult your hairdresser before you visit your milliner! As a matter of fact, these new hats not only cling to the head like a burr, but have a mysterious way of shrinking to half their normal size the moment they are removed from the head. And the reason is quite simple—they are made of elastic.

• • • • • • • •

But from their appearance you would never guess it. The material which is used might be a plain chenille fabric or a crêpe with a contrasting outstanding rib, but beneath, cunningly woven, are the fine elastic threads which put this type of hat among the novelties of 1933.

It is this elastic which makes it the ideal headgear for any kind of spectator sports as well as for cruising—in not too hot weather—and for holiday wear. Nothing less than a storm or a cyclone, it seems to me, will remove it.

MATALASSE silk and little white plumes are used for the hat on the left, which is ideal for those occasions when everything depends on correct accessories. The helmet shape gives a touch of formality, and the plumes which bind the brim and spread over the crown accentuate it.

Twisting to a gnome-like point atop of the crown, the model in chenille on the extreme right is another version of the elastic cap. A turned-up cuff above the forehead softens the line. These elastic hats can be arranged on the head to suit the individual wearer.

HAIR MODES go GREEK

Very "Greek and Gladys-Cooperish is this elegant coiffure for the evening, with its crowning roll of curls and its emphasis on the pretty ear.

DAY COIFFURES remain simple, but in the evening your hair should be your crowning glory.

You can have your own hair set in the Grecian manner, or if you prefer it you can buy detachable rolls and curls for evening "wear."

Lacquer is less in evidence than it was last season.

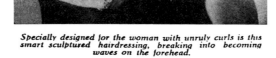

Specially designed for the woman with unruly curls is this smart sculptured hairdressing, breaking into becoming waves on the forehead.

Here is the Jane Austen coiffure, modestly hiding the ears with perpendicular rolls, but revealing the young and lovely forehead. Note the centre parting here and in the first picture. (Antoine).

♦♦

WHAT'S NEW for CHRISTMAS

By Our Shop Detective

A HUGE bronze hairpin — the newest gadget for holding the woollen sports scarf in place. Very chic.
. . . . . .

Bracelets made of three strands of large glass beads, in the rich velvet tones of wine, amethyst and ruby.
. . . . . .

Chromium manicure set on a stand; needs no cleaning. Also nigger leather pochette fitted with enamel powder case. Christmas presents that are useful and attractive.
. . . . . .

Evening belt in plaited silver with coral-colour ring and bar fastening.

A new version of the hair-band in flexible gold. Would be chic with a dark fur wrap for theatre wear.
. . . . . .

Long mittens in black and white net with ruffled tops, also in white satin and fur cloth. Wearing these mittens you have all the "finish" that only long gloves give, and can still show your lovely rings.
. . . . . .

Bag in black enamel and chromium—very new and unusual. Will be smart with a "classic" tailor suit.

Shoulder flower in red fish-net and black organdi—a gay touch on a black satin dinner-dress.
. . . . . .

Dressing gown in flame chiffon velvet, cut on severe tailored lines.
. . . . . .

Evening bag made like an old-fashioned knitted purse in gold tissue sewn with rubies, contrasting with a flat square pochette in gold kid.
. . . . . .

Brown suède belt with big square buckle in dark and light unpolished wood; another brown suède belt has a heavy steel fastening like a curb-chain. Either of these would look good on a beige corduroy sports ensemble.

DRESS·SHOW NOTEBOOK

By
Victoria Chappelle

MOST women will like the new short, fitting jacket shown everywhere in Paris. One house is making them in old-fashioned striped silk with plain cloth skirts, and there are some charming models in black sequins worn with black woollen dresses with sequin trimmings. There is hardly a designer who has not seen the possibilities of evening jackets in gold lamé, and there are several quilted models.

It is doubtful whether the jackets with fur sleeves or those with contrasting material sleeves will find much favour, but there were some with a plain back and sleeves allied to a striped front which not only had the charm of novelty but were becoming into the bargain.

* *

CAPES are by no means dead, although they are hip-length instead of shoulder-length now—not that this makes them easier to wear! Interesting evening wraps by Lelong are made on the lines of Florentine cloaks, with a slightly draped hood at the back, a little fitting bodice beneath, and long, fur-lined slits for the arms. A little green brocade 18th-century jacket matches the brocade top of a black satin Mainbocher frock, and Schiaparelli shows a circular cape of her new padded silk mounted on crinoline. This has a tiny upstanding collar with close-set buttons from neck to hem. Raccoon fur is used for the skirt of another of her evening cloaks, which has a bodice of white padded silk.

* *

EVENING silhouettes provide contrasts. Lanvin has a black velvet gown falling off the shoulders, with a broad silver stitched lamé bertha, a fitting bodice, and a wide skirt gathered at the waist. On the other hand, Mainbocher shows slim princess gowns cut to a point in front and disclosing a hem of pleated net or lace, the décolletage outlining the bust. Another house shows straight tube dresses, spreading at the hem, while Chanel has a bewildering variety of outlines.

Trains are very definitely back again. They may be disguised as drapery. Augustabernard does this by using the material widthways instead of lengthways for a straight skirt and gathering it at the back in folds. And there are one or two "fish-tails."

ON the princess coat on the left a narrow fur stole is used as a collar, tied in a bow with ends hanging to the hem. The jacket of the suit on the right has sleeves of flat fur.

54

OVERHAULING YOUR WARDROBE

Even Tailored Suits are Bargains Now

By Odette

NOW is the time to take thorough stock of your wardrobe, and to fill all those gaps in it while the sales are on and prices are low. Of course, there are some women who refuse to shop at sale-time, saying that they cannot get what they want.

For instance, I have often been told by women who like plain, well-cut tailor-mades that such garments are not reduced in price.

If this was ever the case, it certainly is not true now. At the present moment one can see beautifully tailored suits and blouses at almost half the usual prices, while really exclusive accessories such as scarves, ties, and belts in attractive designs are available at rates that before Christmas would have applied only to the cheapest makes.

Apart from the ready-made departments, it is possible to pick up lengths of tweed and cloth of superb quality that can be made up into suits, odd skirts, jackets, and waistcoats by any of the many excellent " little " tailors that now specialise in making up their customers' own material. I have drawn at the top of the sketch a tailored ensemble that could be made from remnants of good cloth and tweed.

The sketch below this shows another wardrobe " overhaul "—a way of using up a very short length of very good material to excellent effect. Five-eighths of a yard of 36in. or 39in. material would be enough to face the brim of a hat and line a scarf of this kind. Below this again is an entirely new design for the woman who has hitherto found ermine velvet too expensive. The fronts cross over and tie in a knot at the back

of the neck. One yard of 48in. fur fabric or ermine velvet will make this wrap.

Women who do not like cutting out or fitting will be glad to know that one of the most popular wraps of a leading Paris house is a straight length of black or grey ermine velvet (40in. long by 22in. wide) lined with the same ermine velvet in white.

The lowest sketch shows how gracefully this can be worn for day or evening occasions.

Finally, I have given you an idea of how to renovate an old dress by introducing new sleeves, collar, and belt of completely different material. If the sleeves are sufficiently important-looking, the dress will take on quite a new look.

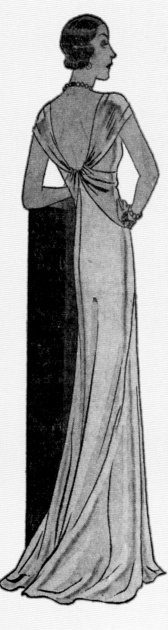

SMART WOMEN are WEARING in PARIS

Brief Capes   Longer Skirts
All-Plaid Accessories

By DARIER

HUNDREDS upon hundreds of styles, many of them conflicting, have been shown at the dress collections. Out of these a certain definite few will survive and become the modes of the season. And why? Just because women like them, buy them, and wear them!

So if you want to be in the vanguard of fashion, watch the smart women. I've been watching the smartest women in Paris, and in this article I propose to report to you the leading modes they are sponsoring.

Where All Agree

Already they have adopted enthusiastically for street wear the woollen coat-dress or frock with shallow detachable cape. Every dressmaking house reports an unprecedented demand for models of this type, and, working in almost uncanny unison, every collection shows a vast choice in just this sort of costume.

An interesting version of this style is the contrasting cape, for which a brilliant colour in thin woollen fabric, such as scarlet or bright green, is used with a flat purse made of the same material. The vivid cape and purse complete a black or dark-coloured woollen frock. I have seen several cape-boleros with flaring elbow-length sleeves worn with tailored wool or silk frocks.

For present southern wear and for later on in town, women are choosing little printed crêpe capes with deep backs that merge into long sash ends to tie about the waist. These are worn over one-toned frocks. Great favour is shown, too, for printed crêpe frocks for afternoon wear with short woollen capes in one tone matching the predominating colour of the print. These are lined with the dress print, and frequently are bordered with fox. Some little wool frocks have snugly fitting short capes.

Skirts are being worn longer for daytime. And formal evening models are so long that they settle on the floor all round and very often trail at the back. A charming dress of this type in lustrous white satin is sketched at the top left. It was worn at a recent dinner dance at a leading restaurant.

For formal afternoon wear, skirts that just cover the ankle permit a gradual transition from the shorter tailored frock to the trailing evening gown.

A Worth model in this manner has just been selected by Lady Weymouth. It is of black ciré satin, with long close sleeves topped by shallow puffs of open work done by using flattened tubing made of the satin and working it into a lacy design. The high draped neckline is gathered into a strass clip on the shoulder, and the crushed belt has strass buckles at the side.

To return to street clothes. Suit and ensemble coats are being worn in a variety of styles. The little belted jacket and the barely hip-length, slightly fitted, coatee are the favourites for suits.

Miss Gloria Swanson, who has just sailed for Hollywood, was seen in Paris in a very smart suit of dark blue wool with a white hair-line. The jacket was very short, just atop the hips, and had a wide shoulder line accentuated by " shoulder-trays " and set-in sleeves pleated at the top. With it she wore a white blouse with cowl neckline, and a dark blue knitted wool cap.

WEAR THIS— *If You're SLIM*

By Odette

A NEW type of dress, which enhances the grace of a figure with a slender waist, has had considerable success since it was launched a few weeks ago.

*   *   *

My sketch shows a very good example of this style. The very wide waistband is cut on the bias, and moulds the figure closely from about 2 inches above to at least 3½ inches below the normal line.

This belt is inserted into the dress to avoid any unnecessary bulk. The top part blouses slightly over this band and the skirt fits easily round the hips.

*   *   *

Dart tucks—combining utility with decorative effect—trim the lower part of the blouse and sleeves and the top of the skirt.

The dress fastens in two places — about 6 inches at the back of the neck and at the side of the waistband in front. Short "plaquet holes" extend above and below the band to allow the dress to be easily slipped on and off. Through these holes can be seen a foundation of a contrasting colour.

*   *   *

This particular model is intended to be in pearl beige silk marocain, and is worn under a Persian lamb cloak lined with the same silk. The large muff trimmed with silver fox to match the cloak is one of the season's modes.

Two-Colour Craze
EVENING GOWNS

MANY women are shy of wearing a dark or indeterminate colour in the evening. "It needs too heavy a make-up," is their excuse. But this season dressmakers are trying to solve the problem by introducing a soft and delicate shade near the face. For instance, on a grey dress— and there was a tremendous amount of grey in the mid-season collections — colour in the shape of a sort of diagonal turn-over collar with matching shoulder straps and belt is added. With a black frock, satin or crêpe in a delicate shade of orchid will be used for the shoulder straps, which become part of the bodice drapery in front. Nearly all the new frocks are of the two-colour order. Molyneux uses the narrowest of brown velvet shoulder straps, with matching belt, gloves and shoes, to accentuate the clarity of a white gown, and adds a tiny cape of coq feathers shading from white to brown.

Yet, in spite of the attraction possessed by these duo-shade frocks, I think the loveliest outfit I have seen lately was a velvet gown in deep sapphire blue, with gloves, shoes, and a long and dignified coat in the same velvet. V.C.

Easy-to-Wear....

"SPORTINGS" for the AUTUMN

Raglan
Sleeves
Once More

By VICTORIA CHAPPELLE

THE new corrugated woollen material is used for the frock below, which fastens at the side. The square buttons are specially made in England. The square inset yoke of contrasting woollen has a tiny roll collar.

ATTRACTIVE features of the Dorville model for the early autumn, shown above, are the high - waisted skirt and raglan sleeves. It is made of grey woollen material with a plain surface which contrasts with the faintly striped crinkled crêpe blouse.

ON the woollen jumper above, the new high waistline is suggested by stripes in a contrasting colour. The slightly full sleeves to the elbow and the long cuffs below are points to note.

THE London fashions for early autumn which are already being quietly shown in some of the salons in the West End will appeal immensely to women. They are more adaptable than the fashions of last season, although perhaps they are not quite so jaunty. But, after all, jauntiness appeals to only one section of the women who are searching for becoming clothes. The older woman, who has been neglected of late, will find these new autumn clothes very easy to wear.

With Corselet Skirt

The high waist, for example, need worry no one. There are several ingenious variations of it, and London designers have studied it carefully with the idea of adapting it to suit the English figure. On many models it drops at the back to a little *below* the normal waistline, and some of the belts are adjustable to any figure.

I recently saw at a London house some woollen sports suits having corselet skirts which were cut to a point in front; this buttoned on to a tab of the material on the crêpe blouse. At the back a belt was fitted at the normal waistline over the skirt. Even on some of the jumpers the high waist is stressed in the design. But these are usually more becoming to the younger woman. Her mother will prefer the belted woollen jumpers and jerkins which are shown in nearly every house.

Another fashion which is sure of a welcome is the wrap-over dress, which has definitely arrived this season. It may fasten at the back

if you prefer, but it is easier, and often more attractive, to have the opening in front, with buttons or clips or some patent fastening to add interest and act as trimming.

Another easy-to-wear newcomer is the raglan sleeve, which will be seen morning, noon, and night next season. This is more important, really, than it appears at first sight, for it is one of the reasons why those " jaunty " lines have passed.

With it have arrived the three-quarter coat and the longish jacket which passes the hips, the cleverly set-in yokes and the hundred and one new kinds of fur scarves, " pieces," and capes. On sports and evening wraps this sleeve is usually very loose; but on the morning suit and the afternoon coat it is nearly always cut in such a way that the silhouette looses very little of its trimness.

TO-DAY'S PAPER PATTERN

Design by Odette

FIVE COATS *in* ONE !

Odette

EVERYONE wants a useful light coat for early autumn days —and here is just the thing to meet the case. Designed by Odette, it is the second pattern to be offered in the already successful new *Daily Mail* Paper Pattern Service. Full particulars for obtaining it are given in the opposite page. The price is sixpence, post free.

The coat has the new sleeves set into deep square armholes, and a long scarf collar which can be tied in many different ways. It can be worn hanging loosely from the shoulders, or belted: and you can make it full or three-quarter length.

Five different ways of making up this pattern are shown in Odette's sketch. First on the left is a black satin coat with white crêpe sleeves to match the dress worn with it. (Black and white is the vogue in Paris.) Next you see it in brown tweed lined with

the same material as the jumper. Or you can make an unlined coat longer than the pattern in pink linen to be worn over a black crêpe or satin dress, as shown on the third figure.

Fourth comes a white homespun coat trimmed with machine stitching.

Two coats are even smarter than one this season. In the right-hand picture they are made quite separately—one of red flannel and one of heavy crash—and put on as one coat with both scarves tied together. A good idea for adapting a summer coat to autumn days.

NEWS FROM THE LONDON DRESS SHOWS

By
Victoria
Chappelle

A VELVET hat, cleverly hand worked, with a matching scarf is a new Condor "set."

FASHION has suddenly become less of an autocrat and more of a fairy godmother. If we feel a qualm when we watch willowy mannequins parading in the slimmest of frocks—apparently about half a yard wide at the hem—it is dispelled as we realise the enormous variety of the ideas planned for the new season. The older woman has not been made such a fuss of for years; all kinds of deficiencies in the figure can be hidden, and the plainest gowns may be made exciting with well-thought-out details.

* * *

MOST of us will still have to concentrate on diet, but just in case our will-power is not strong the designers have been thinking out clothes which will help us. One result is the dark skirt and the lighter jacket—an alliance which is worth about a week's fasting. Another is the cape, and a third an adaptation of the swagger coat—not quite so swagger this autumn but still remarkably helpful.

*

THE new plaid blouses, worn with very plain suits in a light shade or in a colour which repeats the ground of the plaid, will appeal to many women. These were very prominent at a very smart London dress show last week, with plaid jacket linings and gloves to match. Matching gloves are still an important item in the fashions shown in London salons, although they are by no means seen so much outside.

* * *

ONE of the newcomers which are eager to make themselves popular is the suit with the jacket cut like a blouse. It has been nicknamed the 11 to 7 suit, because it can be worn from morning to evening. Then there is the little shoulder cape which looks a trifle top-heavy because it is pulled back in a kind of hood. The wrap-over skirt which fastens at the back with three or four clips—guaranteed to stand any amount of pull—is another.

* * *

IF your bank balance simply will not run to fur this season, make the best of it with a scarf. Worn with a suit, it might match your blouse, and with a wool frock a cashmere scarf in a contrasting shade can be pulled through a couple of slots cut in front. The hanging ends might be fringed, if you like that kind of thing.

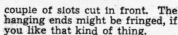

GLOVES to match the spotted wool tunic gown are worn with the Peter Russell outfit above. The plain coat matches the little quill-trimmed hat. On the left is a Jeanne Lanvin hood cape worn with a skirt fastened at the back with clips.

FRIVOLOUS FROCKS
for *Christmas*

By
VICTORIA CHAPPELLE

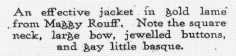

An effective jacket in gold lamé from Maggy Rouff. Note the square neck, large bow, jewelled buttons, and gay little basque.

THERE is just time now, before Christmas parties begin, to look at our frocks, make necessary alterations and adjustments, and decide what will be the smartest little indoor wrap to wear.

Something a little romantic seems to fit in to a Christmas background—frills and ruffles and those new coronets which look so well on a shining head. I have given you two suggestions in this page for a party frock.

The black net gown, as you see it, is the kind of thing for a party which is guaranteed not to be too riotous. But the gown next to it has the simple lines to which no damage can be done. And notice the "boa" of ostrich feather which is carried across the front.

❖ ❖ ❖

IT looks like being very chilly this Christmas, so do not hesitate, if you feel the cold, to wear a frock with long sleeves.

You will be as smart as your neighbour in her backless gown, so long as you remember that a glimpse of your shoulders must be shown even if your arms are not, and that a fairly low back décolletage is necessary.

And here is another idea for the older woman who dislikes going out in the evening because she feels that her gown is not warm enough.

Wear a sleeved jacket with it, made on the newest lines — you will see an example in this page—and interline the sleeves and back with domette, that wafer-thin woollen which is one of the warmest materials imaginable.

For a Girl

I FIND nowadays that the average girl who is looking forward to wearing her first evening dress likes something dignified. Her mother got excited about filmy chiffons and tulle, but *she* prefers a thick satin, moiré, or even velvet.

Still, her dress should not be elaborate, so here is a suggestion which may be helpful. Have the dress made on princess lines, fitting snugly to the figure but not shelving in at the back, with just enough fullness given to the skirt to enable her to dance with comfort.

The neckline in front should be straight from shoulder to shoulder. At the back it may be cut in a modified cowl, or in an oval, or have a couple of wide straps criss-crossed. But the only decoration would be in the little wing sleeves, which should be piped with thick padding, row over row. The effect above rounded young arms is charming.

If white is worn, coloured accessories look well. The gloves should be bought first, in velvet, moiré, satin, or suède, and white shoes dyed to match. This is not expensive. If pos-

A "boa" of dark brown ostrich feathers crossing the corsage of the pale gold velvet Chanel gown shown above makes an unusual trimming.

On the left is a débutante gown in filmy black net with ruchings on the spreading skirt and charming little sleeves. The high front neck-line accentuates the jewelled neck and back straps.

sible, some material to match the gloves in colour and texture should be bought for a pochette. Otherwise, a white one can be carried. This kind of "s e t" would make rather a good Christmas present.

❖ ❖ ❖

WE are seeing many low décolletages this season. But if you dislike them and are thinking of having a frock made for Christmas, why not follow the example of a woman I saw the other day who had had a couple of long oblong slits cut in the back of her frock on each side of her spine?

"Glove sleeves" would look attractive, too. These are merely long sleeves which stop about five inches below the shoulder and are kept up by means of elastic gussets, which can be hidden beneath a kind of cuff. These, however, do look a little elaborate, so unless your frock is perfectly plain, do not think of them. But this suggestion would help to solve the problem of the woman with too thin arms.

Newest HATS
...*at All Angles*

by Odette

IF you are very young and beautiful, or have the type of face that is *supposed* to go with a sweet nature, you should certainly get a hat like the first one on the left. If you depend more on smartness for your effects, this felt hat with its "cockscomb" cut brim will be a better choice.

The hat below, trimmed with long, flexible quills, is for the woman of any age who likes good lines and quiet distinction.

ANY woman who wears an off-the-brow hat just because it is "the latest" has only herself to blame for the result if it does not suit her.

These hats were launched by their designers not with the purpose of sweeping all other types of headgear right out of fashion, but to give everyone a chance of wearing the most becoming hat and still being right up to date.

There are numbers of equally new styles—that may be tilted forward or sideways or worn straight—on show at the best modistes in Paris and London to-day.

New versions of the forward-tilted beret are featured everywhere. Brimmed hats—tilted forwards and slightly sideways—are more favoured than ever among really discriminating women.

A perfect hat for the smart middle-aged woman has put in an appearance since the much-discussed off-the-brow hats made their stir. It has a brim that is turned sharply up at one side to show the hair, with an equally sharp sweep down on the other side, where the brim rolls outwards and downwards till it nearly touches the shoulder

The upturned side hugs the crown and follows the line of the head closely.

HATS that Change Your Character

By *Victoria Chappelle*

A BRIGHT touch of colour on a dark sports hat makes all the difference to your outfit. Here is a brimmed hat in rough felt, tilted at a smart angle, and with a folded crown, giving a pointed effect, finished by white and orange tassels.

*T*IE up your draped cap as though it were a parcel this autumn. Above is a green fancy woollen " glengarry " folded round with satin ribbon in the newest way.

*T*HIS formal Le Monnier afternoon hat of felt and taupé carries out the same idea. The cuff brim of taupé broadens at the back round the felt crown, and the straps across the top are caught in a clip.

*O*UR hat-boxes, far more than our beauty boxes, will contain all we need for several changes of character this season.

* * *

*T*HE first " buy," of course, is a beret. For morning it is big and floppy and severely plain; for afternoon it is just as big, but kept in its place, more often than not, by means of stiffening. Add a few ostrich feather tips and nothing more formal could be found.

* * *

*F*OR those who can stand a rather hard line, or for the days when we are at the top of our form, there are the new little caps made somewhat on the lines of a glengarry but tied up on top, rather like a parcel, with a ribbon or a band of the material. This is for the more sophisticated woman, so if you are very *ingenue*, it is best to avoid it.

* * *

*T*HEN, of course, there are the brimmed hats which all of us need for those days when, for some reason or another, nothing goes right. They have just enough brim to give us back our self-confidence, but it must be subtly curved if the cure is to be complete.

* * *

*F*OR those days when you feel tailored and energetic there are felt sports hats, or the new stiffly brimmed sailors in felt or hatter's plush.

* * *

*V*ELVET, of course, is *the* material this year—luckily for all of us. There is no other so softening, so easy to match or to blend with.

Feathers in any shape or form are at the top of their class for trimmings. Tuck them away at the back or on the top of the crown if they are fluffy, lay them on the crown if they are flat, or let them sweep over your eyebrows if your looks will stand it.

with an eye to CHRISTMAS

RINGS in pink, green, and amber unbreakable crystal, packed in a little glass box. All ready for Christmas morning!

* * *

Powder bowl in the new flat shape, and scent or lotion bottle in "smoky" glass to match.

* * *

Hats for a "cruising Christmas" in fine panama, and an attractive beret for the same purpose in white leather.

* * *

A cocktail set—tiny hat, necklace, and bracelet, all made in twisted strands of gold thread.

* * *

Mulberry kid gloves with gauntlets of plaited strips of felt in mulberry and beige; can be had in nigger and beige.

* * *

Necklace of wooden beads in dull red, green, and natural, tied at the back with narrow ends of suède, together with wooden stud earrings and a two-headed beret pin. This makes an unusual set, and will go well with a suit of "country gentlewoman's" tweeds.

* * *

Long pearl necklace with huge jade and diamanté motif.

* * *

J u m p e r h a n d - k n i t t e d in burnt orange. Has a long scarf that c a n b e d r a p e d and folded in many w a y s, a n d polished wood buttons.

* * *

Veils are important again. With their help we can face the "off the brow" hats. The newest ones are short and very stiff.

Gold or silver kid mules hand-painted in tiny floral design—a charming Christmas present.

* * *

Transparent bracelets in shades of orchid and pink—lovely with the fashionable silver lamé.

* * *

After the wine shades—ruby. Necklace, bracelet, rings and

HERE *are two headdresses seen in the shops—one a simple silver band, the other a little w r e a t h of shell flowers.*

Our Shop Detective

Has

Seen...

earrings are all to be had in this warm clear colour, cleverly set with diamanté.

* * *

L a r g e envelope-shaped pochette in mulberry tweed with chromium fastening.

* * *

Bracelets of leather on steel—very effective in white.

* * *

Hat in nigger satin, with square crown and stitched peak brim, to be worn off the face and slightly tilted to the right. This is an advance model and gives some idea of what we may expect in the spring.

* * *

Apple green crêpe evening bag finely embroidered in diamanté. Also an oval bag in black antelope, fastened by a big jade button.

* * *

The smallest portable gramophone—folds up like a camera and has a green lacquer finish.

* * *

Feather flowers for decora-

***T**HESE elegant evening gloves, more like p u l l - o n sleeves t h a n t h e usual shaped mittens, are very effective in black chiffon—a shop "snapshot."*

tion—amusing and gay in most unnatural shapes and colours!

* * *

Bag and scarf in Scotch tweed —a present for the "country cousin."

* * *

Lamp and shade cleverly painted in boxing scenes—for a man's room.

SMART TRIMMINGS

MONKEY fur is back again in the guise of ingenious trimmings. Since black with white, black with grey, or black with string colour are three of the season's smartest alliances, this light and glossy fur lends itself to admirable effects.

The upper sketch on the right shows an elbow-length cape of monkey fur tied at the shoulder with a lacquered satin ribbon. A wide "bow" of the fur, matching the fringe of fur on the gauntlet gloves of black antelope, is worn by her companion.

THE possibilities of white organdi for evening have not yet been exhausted, and one of the most charming summer accessories is the organdi boa which can be worn over practically any type of gown. On the left you see a pale yellow boa cut in chrysanthemum petals closely massed.

A boa in one circular piece which is slipped over the head and draped carelessly over the shoulders is shown in the lower sketch. It is composed entirely of circular ruffles cut from white organdi.

MY PARIS DRESS SHOW
NOTEBOOK

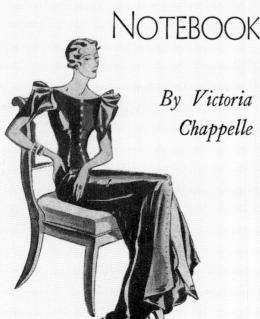

By Victoria Chappelle

ONE is forcibly reminded of mid-Victorian upholstery —as seen in portraits of the period—when looking at some of the materials in the present dress collections.

The striped velvets — sometimes in two colours—and the satins which are being used for some of the new frocks and jumpers might have been copied from those rather dreary fabrics. They are not particularly becoming — but Paris obviously thinks them worth while !

SQUARE shoulders will share their importance next season with small square cape-collars. These are running through the collections like an epidemic. Whether in material and edged with fur, or in a flat fur-like astrakhan, the principle is nearly always much the same—the collar is drawn up close to the neck and then fluted over the shoulders and along the back and the front. The same idea is achieved with a long strip of fox fur occasionally.

IT is interesting to note how many designers have determined to do without lavish fur this year. In consequence, some of the less formal coats have a good deal more interest about the neckline. Elizabethan ruffles in the coat material, padded rolls, rows of piping, or scarves made of plaided strips of the material are among the intelligent efforts made to solve the problem.

Glove interest has waned considerably. It is true that one house uses three-quarter sleeves with long fur-gauntleted gloves, but this is an isolated case. Gloves of green tweed to match a coat and frock, which,

WHAT YOU WILL WEAR

this AUTUMN & WINTER

The Paris Dress Shows
Sketched by————
© ODETTE ©

A "tube" dress with skimpy train and enormous shoulder bows.

black panne

pale grey net with rose velvet sash

a new glove

bottle green moire

There is plenty of diversity where the evening silhouette is concerned

Belts which button to the dress instead of meeting

Silver fox on beige cloth

Persian lamb sleeves and border on black velvet coat

⅔ length coats with full backs over straight narrow skirts in darker shade of same

Short belted jacket with dropped shoulders and full sleeve

A "classic" redingote worn with a net jabot note the pockets

Costumes may have short, medium or full length coats

Monkey fur on white velvet

Linen collars trimmed with strips of ravelled linen. Loose, high necks are still good

Capes do not flare

Widest below the shoulder line

Tied at back of neck

Gloves match wraps

Three new corsage treatments

A Vionnet model in ermine

Large sleeves on small coat with wide fur cuffs

Short fur wraps for wearing over dresses or plain cloth coats

The millinery excitement of the moment is Suzanne Talbot's "Bersagliere"

The Tudor ruffle is an American inspiration that has found favour in Paris

Evening wraps

COATS Must Have FUR

By
Victoria
Chappelle

A NEW way of suggesting shoulder width is shown by the manner in which the mink trimming is added to the sleeves of the brown cloth coat on the left above—an idea which is accentuated by the luxurious shawl collar. Next to it is a new Patou version of the highwayman coat. The cape is part of the coat, which is buttoned up to the neck, while a fur collar stands away from the shoulders and continues as a border on the cape.

HOW a coat can be closely furred almost to the waist and yet have a slim line is shown by the Mainbocher model in the third picture. Brown caracul is worked on the top and sleeves of the brown burlap weave coat; even the buttons are fur. The shoulder trimming of Japanese mink on the last model can be easily removed when the wearer tires of it. The collar is a new upstanding one, and can be pulled up round the face or dropped back.

FUR will be the keynote on smart winter coats. Whether it is real or not need not worry you so much—furriers have achieved miracles this year in disguising bunny and sheep—as whether it is placed in the way which becomes you best.

If you are thin, for instance, play up this new fullness about the shoulders and top of the arm for all you are worth. Choose long-haired furs. You want a soft frame for your face. Fox is your obvious choice, but if this is too much for your pocket, foxaline will look quite as attractive. But both are delicate—although fox will, of course, last longer—so give them plenty of attention. Shake the collar carefully before and after wearing, and comb it occasionally with a fur comb. If you have a good fox fur and want to cherish it—you will find it is apt to get woolly where it rubs against the neck—a good plan is to have it mounted as a border on a shoulder-wide collar of material, so that it can

be thrown back on the shoulders when you do not need warmth, or pulled up round the neck when the wind is chilly.

If, on the other hand, you are—well, a little more than plump, you will be wise to forswear the luxuriousness of fox furs, or any long-haired fur, at least for the day-time. Flat furs will make you look slimmer and elegant, and you will find astrakhan, Persian lamb, the cheaper astrakhan paw, and their many imitations excellent for you, especially in black. I am sorry I cannot suggest any other line but that of the long rever if you want to add apparent inches to your height, although the actual collar need not be flat. But sleeves *must* be unfussy.

The rest of us have so wide a choice this season that we are likely to suffer from an embarrassment of riches. Most economical is the loose scarf collar, which can be made up in several ways. You can tie the ends, or cross them and button them trimly below each shoulder, or pull them through

a crystal or coloured bracelet-ring, as was done on a coat I saw at Whiteleys' dress show. You can have your scarf cut on cowl lines and wear it with the hood effect at the back, or turn it back to front and have the fullness beneath your chin.

This type of thing really comes within the category of the separate "fur piece," which nearly all the fashion houses are showing just now. So does the little cape cut square, round, or to a point back and front, which can be whipped off and worn with two or three coats.

Chilly mortals who dread winter will find comfort in the deep fur yoke, which wanders over the top of the sleeves and usually has a high, cosy collar. On the newly opened fashion floor at Waring and Gillow's I was shown a coat of this kind with a scarf almost deep enough to pull up round the ears. The usefulness of a wide shawl collar, too, can be doubled by leaving the longer end unstitched and merely buttoning it to the coat. On a chilly day this end—which has been provided with a

long thread loop—can be taken up to the shoulder and fastened there.

Trimming Not Essential

Sleeve trimmings are important on new winter coats, although they are not essential. If you are sure they suit you, pieces of fur placed just below the shoulders are the easiest way of getting the broad effect; otherwise they are things to avoid. Many houses, however, compromise by stitching these on in such a way that they can be easily removed when you are tired of them. Far more subtle in effect are the bands stitched in an oval and lined or edged with flat fur to match the collar. Some clever coats of this kind were seen at Harrods' parade.

If you want breadth but don't want the sleeves to be prominent, try the effect of a small fur cape which is gathered a little round the neck. This must be attached to the coat to get the right line

A new type of fur-trimming for the perfectly plain coat is the stole made on much the same lines as those so popular in the nineteen-hundreds. The modern woman, however, prefers a little less lavishness, and simply wears her fur in a throttle collar round her neck, leaving two long ends to fall to the hem of her coat.

Beauty

In the 1930s the Daily Mail had a 'Beauty Critic', Joan Beringer, who judged the make-up and hairstyles of fashionable women-about-town with an unforgiving eye. At a dance she sees a charming, pretty girl with parted, deep-coral lips, "But the arm that lay against the man's black coat was a muddy yellow - that depressing hue that comes when sun-tan is slowly fading," and, horrors, "the fingernails were varnished a muddy orange". She cannot excuse another woman wearing rich plum shades: "She should have set about getting her skin thoroughly bleached; failing this she should have obliterated the tan patches with disguising cream". Her critical notices come with plenty of stern advice. "One part white wine vinegar to three parts distilled water will get rid of freckles ..." "If you are not wearing gloves during the warm spells, devote a few extra minutes daily to your manicure ... Remember to wash your powder puff more frequently in the summer". In winter, zinc and castor oil is a good remedy for chapped hands, along with a little hand jelly(not inferior soaps). There are exhortations on rolling the eyes to keep them young, and on mouthwashes: "Look around you: is it not remarkable to see a woman over 40 who has a whole mouthful of healthy teeth?" Short white hair is the new rage (displacing platinum blondes), as are artificial Greek curls, stuck on the hair either side of the forehead. Above all, exercise away those wrinkles, headlines Joan. "Get that Clean-Cut Chin Line (Tip-Tilted Hats Demand It)".

GET *that* CLEAN-CUT CHIN LINE

Tip-tilted Hats Demand It

JOAN BERINGER.

Use an upward movement to cleanse the neck.

Press the backs of the hands firmly against the chin.

The last movement of the third exercise.

Throwing the head well back.

THE success of tip-tilted hats depends to a great extent on one's profile. A good throat and chin line are essential; sagging cheek muscles and the least suspicion of a double chin are revealed and accentuated more and more as the line of the hat is lifted. The newest version of the Marie Stuart hat, recently described by Odette in this page in particular demands a clear-cut chin.

Three Exercises

While facial contour depends to a great extent on massage, much can be done by exercise to preserve and enhance the graceful lines of chin and throat.

The following three exercises, posed by Miss Dodo Watts, the British film star, should be performed in loose clothing in a well-ventilated room every morning, and again immediately before retiring. From five to ten minutes should be given to them each time.

Begin by cleansing the neck and chin thoroughly with a good cleansing cream, using an upward movement towards the ears as shown in the first photograph above. After the cream has been put on in this way, wipe off the surplus with a moistened pad of cotton wool, and massage the neck upwards with the backs of the hands (see second picture). Then perform the following exercises :—

1. Breathe in deeply, bend the head forward, letting it fall on the chest, and breathe out. Relax the muscles. While the head is down, breathe in, stiffen the muscles, slowly raise the head and let it drop backwards as far as possible, as shown by the third photograph. Breathe out, bring the head back to its natural position, and repeat several times.
2. Make the neck muscles tense, breathe in deeply, bend the head sideways to the left, and breathe out. Regain first position, breathe in, bend the head to the right as far as possible, and breathe out. Repeat five times.
3. Breathe in, make the neck muscles tense, turn the head—looking up and over the right shoulder as in the fourth picture—move slowly and turn as far as the muscles will stretch, breathe out. Return to the natural position and repeat the exercise, this time turning the head over the left shoulder. This last exercise is particularly good where the neck is short and thick.

That fleshy lump at the back of the neck that is so disfiguring can also be eradicated by the right exercises. These should be done in addition to the three already described.

Stand erect with the hands on the back of the head, let the chin drop forward on the chest and relax the muscles.

Pull the head upward, letting the muscles at the back of the neck resist the movement, until the head falls as far back as possible.

Drop the head forward on the chest, raise slowly upward, and describe a circle, five times to the right and five times to the left. If there is a slight dizziness between these rotations take a short rest before resuming the reverse movements.

Friction massage with a stiff, dry loofah across the back of the neck will help considerably to reduce superfluous flesh at that part.

Three Easy Exercises... *for* SLIMNESS & BEAUTY

*T*HE "two piece" worn by the demonstrator ensures freedom at the waist.

First is a version of the "touch-the-toes" exercise. Fling yourself up on tip-toe—and bend till the hands touch the floor.

Take things slowly at first! "Ten times each in rapid succession" is a rule which cannot be followed until you are proficient.

*A*FTER the touch-the-floor movement, do the exercise shown above. Sit on the floor with legs stretched out, face forwards, and raise the arms to shoulder level. Then swing the body round to right and left.

The third exercise is shown in the centre picture. Keep the sitting position, but instead of raising the arms, put the palms flat on the floor. Then raise yourself as shown.

WHAT'S WRONG with YOUR MAKE-UP?

By JOAN BERINGER

OUR beauty critic has recently attended the smartest London first-nights and dance restaurants, and her expert eye has detected several little faults in make-up—even among the most chic of women. And, of course, it is tremendously helpful to read about them, so as to avoid them yourself!

IN the crowded foyer at an ultra-fashionable "first night" I noticed a woman with a long, rather thin, face. She was not unattractive ... but she had chosen staring white powder, and in the centre of either cheek was a hard-edged patch of rouge.

This woman's rouge was of the compact type, and was wrongly applied over too light a powder. Cream rouge, especially as her skin was obviously inclined to be dry, would have been the better choice. On this long face it should have been sparingly used and blended well away from the nose outwards towards the temples. It should have been well worked into the skin with the finger-tip *before* powdering, and the edges "faded out" with the help of a face tissue. A faint touch of rouge on the tip of the chin and at the lobes of the ears would have made her face seem shorter.

Before making up the lashes, brush them with a trace of eyelash cream.

A girl's charming face looked at me over the shoulder of her dancing partner. She had a pretty coral and cream make-up; parted, deep-coral lips. But the arm that lay against the man's black coat was a muddy yellow—that depressing hue that comes when sun-tan is slowly fading. The finger-nails were varnished a vivid orange ...

A LITTLE liquid powder in a creamy shade, or a waterproof cream smoothed into her skin, would have made this girl's arms as lovely as her face. A few minutes' trouble would have changed hands that looked as if they were dirty into pale hands, coral tipped. The nails should have harmonised with her lipstick instead of quarrelling violently with it!

* * *

With a white dress and black sleek hair, another woman started the evening with an effective bronze make-up—vivid lipstick, vert-green eyeshadow with grey-green eyes, and green mascara. So far so good.

Towards the early hours, alas, her nose was shiny, and her powder had gone into dark streaks through constant "retouching." Her mouth had a plastered look, from the frequent use of lipstick during the evening.

THIS woman should have made use of a bronzing lotion for her foundation or, as her skin was greasy, of a liquid powder in a bronze shade. She should then have powdered lightly, first with a pale powder, then with sun-tan. Streaks would then have been avoided, especially if, for hand-bag use, she had blended the two powders carefully together. To make her lipstick stay intact, when making up, she should first of all have powdered her lips, then applied lipstick. When dry, she should have powdered over again and given her lips a second application. Or, if she had thought of it, she might have used a liquid lip colouring under her ordinary lipstick.

MY FIRST BEAUTY TREATMENT

By A Woman of Forty

"Relaxed muscles and a flabby condition of the skin," was the beautician's diagnosis. As she massaged I heard her murmur that I suffered from acidity, and she then recommended plenty of lemon juice in hot water *without* sugar.

My skin, apparently, was too soft, while the muscles around the jawbone had slackened, giving me a tendency to double chin and wrinkles. My greatest need was for toning up, and this my assistant proceeded to do with vigour.

After cleansing, a thorough massage with magnolia night cream. Plenty of pressure below the chin and jawbone.

With muslin soaked in skin tonic and a few drops of astringent wrapped round a patter, the work of strengthening my muscles proceeded. My neck, chin, jaw, and forehead were all patted smartly, while my whole face tingled in response. "You should allow ten minutes for doing this every night," I was told, "and as often as you can spare half an hour give yourself a 'tie-up.'"

The "tie-up" is a simple home treatment. Large pads of cotton wool are soaked in skin tonic, with astringent on

the one which is placed below the chin. These are laid over the whole face and neck—eyes and nose excepted—over a layer of wrinkle cream, and a band is then tied firmly beneath the chin and over the top of the head.

After my assistant did this she dabbed a block of ice over my chin and jawbone, up in front of my ears, and over my forehead. Then I was left to rest.

SEEN ON THE BEAUTY COUNTERS

FOUR new creams in fancy jars, fitting into deep green boxes which are ornaments to the dressing-table. Orange skin food in a jar resembling an orange, a lemon cleansing cream similarly packed, and a powder cream in a jade jar are all 3s. 6d. each, while a hand cream in a turquoise jar is 2s. 6d.

Feminine beauty boxes in three perfumes. One, costing 6s. 9d., contains day cream, powder, complexion soap, and a pencil with eyebrow cosmetic at one end and lipstick at the other.

An extra strong bleach for removing discoloration of the skin. This is made into a paste, smoothed on the skin, and allowed to dry thoroughly. Remove with the finger-tips and stroke in gently a little nourishing oil.

A wrinkle jelly glaze which is spread all over the face and allowed to remain on all night. The face must be kept perfectly still while the jelly is drying, and this must be quite dry before retiring. Remove in the morning with a skin lotion.

COOL BEAUTY for AUGUST

By JOAN BERINGER

MANY women use the same make-up, the same heavy creams and powder bases, winter and summer. But the woman who is complexion-conscious would no more follow such an unintelligent and uncomfortable procedure than she would dream of wearing a fur coat on a hot August day.

Our friends the chemists and the beauty experts have preparations which help on the charitable work of keeping us not only looking but feeling as cool as the water lily in the most grilling of heat waves.

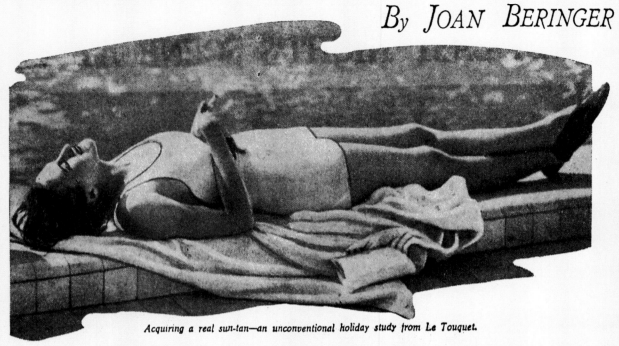
Acquiring a real sun-tan—an unconventional holiday study from Le Touquet.

Frequent Make-up

A treatment which is as refreshing as a plunge into a deep pool is being given at one famous salon.

After a thorough cleansing with a light cream, pads of cotton wool soaked in iced water and a cooling lotion are laid over eyes and mouth. Over these again, thin porous cloths wrung out of icy-cold water are placed, covering face and neck, and a lotion made from marigolds is sprinkled over the cloths. The result is deliciously cool, and the treatment is so simple that it can be easily carried out by oneself at home when one has a few minutes to spare.

In hot weather, to avoid clogging the pores should be our greatest concern. So make-up must be renewed more often. It is a mistake at all times to put fresh cosmetics over old make-up. Fragrant washes are made from herbs. Liquefying removal creams are now put up in tubes for the handbag, and there is no excuse for any woman not carrying one of these with her. After removal, a dab over with a cooling astringent or eau-de-Cologne is all that is necessary before renewing the make-up.

A lotion that has the finest filtration of powder in its composition—too delicate, this, to be called a liquid powder—is one of the best make-up bases for summer use. It not only protects the skin, but absorbs excessive moisture, only a fine dusting of powder being then necessary.

Rouge, if used at all, should be put on most sparingly. Be more delicate in tone and, for preference, choose a liquid rouge. Dry lips may need a trace of oil or skin food under the lipstick. This is a better method than choosing a lipstick that is very greasy.

There have been so many hints about using a sun-tan powder with a bronzed skin that many women choose far too deep a tone.

Not Too Dark

Powder, even with a sun-tan make-up, should not be nearly as dark as the tan make-up foundation, as the powder tends to darken on the skin, especially if the puff is frequently in action. Have your handbag powder a tone lighter than that in your bowl on the dressing-table, and avoid that dark yellowish or streaky look round nose and mouth. Your bronze powder can be toned to a nicety by mixing in some rachel or naturelle.

For the fair English skin that cannot tan with safety, or for the cream and roses girl who wishes to remain her exquisite self, there is a new sun-proof cream that actually deflects the sunlight. This is used once or twice during the day as a powder foundation.

The girl on holiday who has acquired the "real thing" in tans needs little or no make-up or protection. She looks best with her own natural glow of health—and so much cooler! A dust of powder on the nose and a vivid lipstick (but carefully applied, please, not just smeared on) will be enough.

Eyes suffer in the heat. They get strained and burned. They should be rested as much as possible, and dark the lashes. If eye shadow is used let it *be* a shadow—a wraith, in fact, of its former self.

Hair must be shampooed frequently. Let frictions play a daily (or rather a nightly) part in keeping our heads cool.

Not only on the beaches but in Bond-street the stockingless and sandalled mode is seen. Women are having their legs treated—bleached or bronzed according to whether their owners are lily-fair or gypsy-brown—and cos-

glasses worn in bright sunlight—a fashionable precaution on smart *plages* this summer. Twice or three times a day is not too often to bathe them. For this, cold tea is delightfully refreshing. Eye make-up should be less exotic if we wish to be cool-looking—a trace of oil on the lids and on the brows, and a touch of mascara for

metics specially made for the legs have arrived.

The legs must be smooth and evenly coloured. Any tendency to redness or goose flesh must be strenuously dealt with. Vinegar and salt (2 or 3 tablespoons of salt to a tumbler of vinegar) added to the bath and a good bleach cream will look after these details. The use of a liquid powder to match the rest of the skin, and of the new leg cosmetic, will give the finishing touch of elegance to this latest fad of fashion.

AN EGG MASK FOR BEAUTY

·······TREATMENT YOU CAN······· DO AT HOME·······

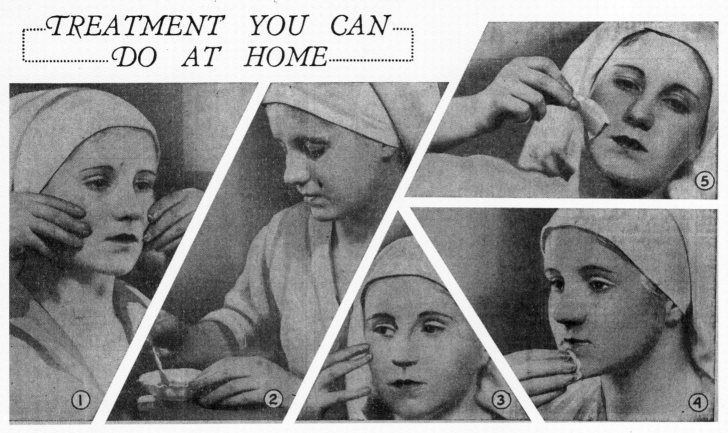

① ② ③ ④ ⑤

SUPPLEMENT the good work of your cleansing and nourishing creams by giving your face an occasional egg mask. It will strengthen the muscles and greatly improve the texture of the skin.

1. *Remove all dust and make-up with cleansing cream. Wipe off thoroughly. Pat muscle oil round the corners of nose and mouth. Wipe off.*
2. *Separate the yolk from the white of one egg. Put white aside and beat the yolk. You will not require the white.*
3. *Spread the beaten yolk quickly and evenly over face and neck with finger tips. Leave to dry in a crust. This should take only a few minutes.*
4. *Remove egg yolk with cotton wool soaked in cold rose-water.*
5. *Pat the face smartly with a pad soaked in astringent before making up as usual.*

Beauty exercises in twelve minutes

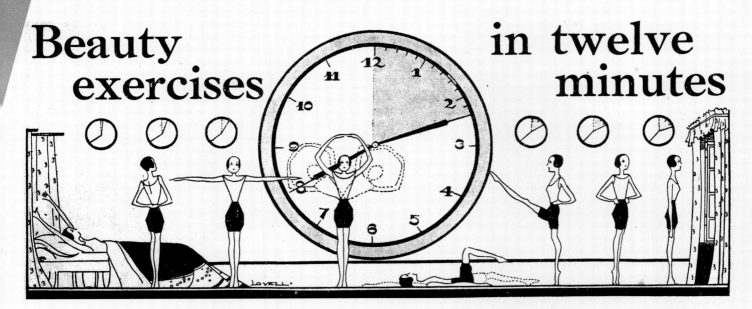

TO keep her figure young and supple should be the aim of every woman, whether she is twenty or fifty, and this can best be done by common-sense diet and the daily exercising

by Joan Beringer

which is so fashionable this winter. The variety of exercises to choose from is bewildering, and in their zeal many women continually chop and change, trying out first this system then that. Now, that is not the right way to go about it. As with creams and lotions for the face, any system, or any specialised exercise, must be given a fair run if results are to be obtained.

In working out a system for the average figure, I have chosen exercises that will do the job assigned to them quickly, easily, and with hundred per cent. efficiency, IF—and it is a very important IF—the routine is faithfully, conscientiously, and regularly carried out.

How long does it take? Study the clock faces above and you will see that when you are proficient the whole set need delay you for only TWELVE MINUTES. And in that time you can exercise *your* whole body, from top to toe.

Before Rising . . . Stretch

(a) With arms at sides, stretch upwards from toes to shoulders, flexing the spine. Relax. Arms out-flung at sides, stretch outwards. Relax. Arms above head, stretch upwards. Relax. Arms at sides, stretch downwards from shoulders to toes. Relax.

(b) Open the eyes wide, and then rotate them rapidly round to the left, then to the right. Stretch the fingers: spread them wide: open and shut them rapidly.

After Rising . . . Exercise

Neck

(a) Stand erect, hands on hips. Drop head, completely relaxed, on chest. Let it drop backwards as far as possible without strain. Let the head, still thrown back, loll first to the right, then to the left. Repeat five times. Back to chest position.

(b) Make a complete circle with head from right to left, five times; from left to right, five times.

Contour

Throw the head back, letting jaw drop open. Close very slowly, pulling strongly against the lower jaw. Do this five times.

Chest and Shoulders

Place the back of one hand in the palm of the other behind the back, just above the waist line. Drop chin on chest, elbows forwards. Press elbows back slowly and strongly: at the same time raise head slowly, inhaling deeply. Do this five times.

Arms

Stretch the arms outwards · at shoulder height, palms downwards, pulling strongly from shoulder muscles right along the arm to the finger tips. Turn arms slowly outwards until palms are uppermost. Repeat five times. Return to first position. Turn the arms *inwards* until palms are uppermost. Repeat five times.

Waist

(a) Stand erect, feet together. Form an arch with the arms above the head, finger tips lightly touching. Bend down as far to the left as possible. Back to first position. Bend down to the right as far as possible. Back to first position. Repeat five times each way. (Keep abdomen flat and lower back well tucked in.)

(b) With the feet slightly apart, stretch the arms above the head, thumbs linked. Keeping the head always at the same level between the arms, describe a circle with the body, using the waist as pivot. Repeat five times to the left; five to the right. (To improve a poor circulation, start this exercise slowly and gradually work · up to a rousing speed.)

Below Waist

(a) Lie on the floor with knees bent, feet on the ground, arms at sides. Raise the knees as high as pos-sible until you feel (and look) like a trussed chicken. Straighten and lower the legs as slowly as in a slow motion picture, at the same time raising the arms above the head and flexing the spine. Repeat three times, relaxing between each movement and breathing deeply. (This exercise is fairly strenuous; if a strain is felt, it should not be practised too slowly to begin with.)

(b) Lying on the floor, with the arms a little away from the sides, lift the left leg and swing it over to the right until the foot touches the ground. As the left leg returns to first position, swing the right leg over to the left. Repeat ten times, aiming at getting a good rolling movement with the hips.

Legs

Stand erect, hands on hips. Rise on the balls of the feet. Rise on the left foot and kick as high as possible with the other, changing the feet rapidly with a light hopping movement. (This exercise can be cut out by the not so young and active and be substituted by walking round the room on tip-toe.)

Ankles

(a) Rise and lower repeatedly on the balls of the feet.

(b) Standing on the balls of the feet, rise up on tip-toe, flexing the foot and instep muscles strongly.

Now, with the spine straight, arms at sides, abdomen flattened, lower back well tucked in and shoulders thrown easily back, deep breathe for one minute. Think of the lungs as bellows: expand the ribs outwards, keeping the shoulders level.

And there, in twelve short minutes, is a daily drill which will keep you young and healthy from top-to-toe. Good luck to you!

Beauty Treatments for Busy Women

BUSY women are welcoming a new and inexpensive beauty treatment, designed to make them fresh and spruce without needless waste of time. This treatment takes only twenty minutes, and during that time the face is cleansed and made up, an expert deciding rapidly the exact shade of cosmetics that will suit the client's dress-colouring.

A Continental treatment which is being given in London is intended to take away tired lines and wrinkles, especially from beneath the eyes. Heavy eye pads, soaked in lotion, are put over the eyes, and while the " patient " rests, an orange light plays over her wrinkles: It has the effect of ironing out the tired lines and leaving her rested for the day.

Look Lovely To-day!

A LOTION made of one part white wine vinegar to three parts distilled water will remove that light crop of freckles after a day at the seaside.

Protect Your Eyes

If you are spending a day on the beach, beware the glare of the sea. Take either a brimmed hat, sun-glasses or an eye-shade. The latter are smart in piqué with a green lining, and can be had with or without a net to keep the hair in place. Bathe the eyes when you get home at night in warm water with a pinch of boric powder added.

For the Nose

This prominent member is the first to receive the sun's attention. Even if you let your complexion "go" for the day's outing, treat your nose with vanishing cream, or cream with a powder base. This is available in all smart flesh shades.

An Evening Cocktail

If you have remembered to bring your tube of liquefying cleansing cream, your handbag flask of eau-de-Cologne or astringent, your rouge compact and powder, you can give yourself a facial "cocktail" in five minutes at the end of the day and emerge fresh and fragrant for the evening's amusement.

J. B.

Have You a Film Face?

By a Cinema Director

CYNICS say that the perfect film face is made in the studio beauty parlour! There is plenty of truth in this gibe, for miracles are wrought in our beauty shop. But there is a naturally perfect film face, and when a girl of this rare type walks under the lights for the first time an expert can spot her immediately.

She has a pale skin of fine texture which needs the minimum of make-up. Her hair is auburn—*not* platinum blonde—and has wonderfully effective lights and shadows. Her eyes are dark and sparkling, set rather wide apart, and her brow is low and broad. White, perfectly even teeth are almost essential. But the shape of the mouth does not matter very much, provided it is not ultra wide, for new mouths can very easily be sketched in with lipstick. A delicate nose, no matter whether *retroussé* or Roman, a clear profile, long neck and well-poised head complete my perfect film beauty.

Wide-set eyes and a dazzling smile— Miss Loretta Young, a classic beauty of the films.

Contradictory

Now someone will mention at least a dozen stars in the first rank who are entirely unlike that. I admit that there are many, but each one has some quality, apart from facial beauty, which has made it worth while to spend on her our skill in make-up and lighting. Each has an expressive face which clearly mirrors the personality of the actress. That is almost the only quality which cannot be faked for the screen.

how to have Lovely Teeth

LOOK around you. Is it not remarkable to see a woman over forty who has a whole mouthful of healthy teeth?

That is one of the penalties we must pay for civilisation. And it is a pretty severe penalty, for, apart from the health aspect, white and gleaming teeth are a tremendous asset to beauty.

By the Clock

That is the wrong way to go about this important part of beauty régime. Teeth should be brushed by minutes—two or three minutes, timed by the clock without which no modern bathroom is complete. They should be brushed, not horizontally only (that is the least part of the business), but with a see-saw and rotary movement, starting with the back teeth, near the gums.

The perfect tooth cleanser whitens but does not abrase the enamelled surface of the teeth, and it leaves our mouth feeling as if it had had a deliciously stimulating astringent.

New Toothbrushes

When choosing a toothbrush, unless you are prepared to buy two or three at a time to use them in strict rotation and to treat them to an antiseptic bath at frequent intervals, it is just as well to buy a reliable but not too expensive brand and to discard it after a month's service. This is a far better system than hanging on to a brush long after its value as a cleansing agent has departed.

Civilised woman (at least, she who wants to keep her teeth sound all her life) must try to counteract the deleterious effect of soft living and adulterated food. We can't go back,

A SUNNY smile enhanced by strong, white teeth—a study of Renee Macready, the young English film actress.

it seems, to primitive ways, and gnaw a bone now and then for health and enjoyment, but we can include in a meal some hard and toothsome substitute such as an apple—an apple being a tooth toilet in itself—or a salad of some kind of fruit. Failing that, we can chew a piece of hard toast or a crust. One or other of these simple foods can be present in any average meal.

Professional Aid

One other word—perhaps one which seems hardly necessary in these enlightened days of hygiene. Even if your teeth give you no trouble and you have never had one taken out or stopped in your life, form the habit of paying a three- or four-monthly visit to your dentist and get him to brush and polish your teeth for you.

Hands Up for Winter!

HANDS which during summer keep smooth and white without any trouble have a disconcerting way of developing all sorts of ailments when winter comes.

Some of these ailments are painful; some, such as redness and cold, are just unbeautiful and annoying. But whatever form they take, most of the troubles to which the hands are heir in winter come from one source—faulty circulation.

The obvious remedies for this is sensible clothing and lots of outdoor exercise—not always such easy matters for the town dweller.

Much can be done by devoting a few moments daily to massage and exercise. The hands should be first generously coated with olive or almond oil, or with lanoline thinned out with one of these oils. "Wash" the hands (I mean, use the action of washing the hands) with the cream, and then stroke the fingers vigorously as if you were pulling on and off a pair of tight gloves.

Next, stretch the fingers sideways and longways, and open and close the hands, flexing the muscles strongly.

Zinc and castor oil is an old-fashioned remedy for chapping, and can be obtained ready made up. After washing, a little hand jelly or an emollient should always be rubbed in. Some people use glycerine and wonder why it is not effective. Glycerine should always be applied *while the hands are still damp.*

If you dread having red hands in winter, avoid extremes of hot and cold water, and see that the water is softened. A few drops of spirits of camphor will do this for you and will act as a mild bleach as well. To whiten red hands, keep some toilet oatmeal near by, and rub the hands with it occasionally. The oatmeal can be used sometimes instead of soap.

And now for those arch enemies of hand beauty—chilblains. All the precautions suggested against chapping apply also to chilblains. As far as possible keep the hands warm by natural means, and when coming in from the cold never in any circumstances warm them at the fire or on a radiator. The temptation is great, but the penalty the chilblain subject must pay is greater.

Friction is good as a preventive, and for this purpose alcohol (90 per cent.) can be used. Broken chilblains should not be washed with soap and water, but should be gently soothed with olive oil. A simple dressing that can be used on this painful subject is composed of two grains of iodine with 75 grains of collodion or castor oil.

Before going out on a cold winter's morning, instead of bemoaning your lot, clap your hands and jump for joy for five minutes—even if you do feel depressed! Make that sluggish circulation get to work and keep you warm through the day.

Your LOVELIEST FEATURES are—

HAVE you secretly yearned to possess those large, alluring eyes that are commonly supposed to be very beautiful, regretting your own rather small ones? Or spent hours trying to massage your tip-tilted nose to a straighter and more classical outline?

If so, you can cease both these struggles against Fate, for at least two famous men artists have given it as their opinion that a tip-tilted nose is one of woman's most attractive features, while one, Mr. Malcolm Osborne, the R.A., thinks that small eyes are the loveliest feature a woman can possess!

Well-Set Eyes

In the opinion of this artist, eyes that are smaller than is usually considered beautiful in the conventional sense are generally better set and more in proportion with the rest of the face. Large eyes, he thinks, are less proportionate, and dominate the face too much.

And to cheer those women whose mouths are their despair because they are so big, this artist adds that next to small eyes he would place a large mouth as one of the most attractive features of a woman's face.

"There are character and generosity

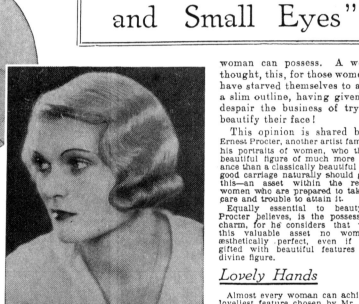

WOMEN with such graceful neck and shoulders as those in the picture above can afford to forget their faces, according to one masculine expert. Others say that the greatest of feminine charms is a retroussé nose.

in the mouth that errs on the large side," he points out. "Small mouths lack character and mobility."

To complete his encouraging and original views on lovely features, he adds that a tip-tilted nose and a slight irregularity in the composition of the face give a charmingly piquant effect which is more appealing, in his opinion, than a classically, regular one.

Not Aquiline Noses

Mr. Gerald Kelly, R.A., thinks that the whole composition of a woman's face and figure is so exquisite and complete that it is almost impossible to say that any one feature is better than another. But he does, most emphatically, dislike an aquiline nose.

"A woman can have a turned-up nose

and still be beautiful, but I loathe a nose that has a hook or a big bridge," he declares vehemently.

A well-set head on a rounded neck and shoulders is more important and lovelier, according to Mr. Melton Fisher, R.A., the portrait painter, than a lovely face—a warning to those women who concentrate on keeping the face young and attractive and neglect the set of the head and the contour of the throat.

Next to this he considers a beautiful figure, even if the face is completely plain, the most valuable asset a

woman can possess. A welcome thought, this, for those women who have starved themselves to achieve a slim outline, having given up in despair the business of trying to beautify their face!

This opinion is shared by Mr. Ernest Procter, another artist famous for his portraits of women, who thinks a beautiful figure of much more importance than a classically beautiful face. A good carriage naturally should go with this—an asset within the reach of women who are prepared to take some care and trouble to attain it.

Equally essential to beauty, Mr. Procter believes, is the possession of charm, for he considers that without this valuable asset no woman is æsthetically perfect, even if she is gifted with beautiful features and a divine figure.

Lovely Hands

Almost every woman can achieve the loveliest feature chosen by Mr. Harold Knight, A.R.A., who considers beautiful hands to be of great importance. In his opinion, slender, supple fingers on a well-turned wrist are a delight to paint and a joy to watch. There are few women who cannot make their hands attractive by exercises and massage such as those described recently in this page.

Another artist, famous for his Academy portraits of Society women, stipulates that to be really beautiful a woman must have slanting grey eyes with a slight fleck of brown in the iris. Next in attractiveness he places brown eyes, "which have a depth and melting softness which is seldom, if ever, found in blue eyes."

Mona Curran

Keep Your EYES Young

SIMPLE TREATMENTS
That Can be Done at Home

by
Jeanne de Maury

A REST for tired eyes is shown above. Soak pads of lint as directed in the article, and hold them over the eyes.

To keep the brows shapely, brush them into a well-defined line with an eyebrow brush and a little brilliantine, removing any straggling hairs with tweezers (see top picture).

THE daily eye-bath is one of the most important items in your home beauty-treatment. Tilt the head slightly back, as shown above.

On the left—clear, alert eyes and smooth skin are the result of persisting with daily eye-drill.

EYES show the strain of life before almost any other feature. Prematurely sunken eyes, tired lids, lines, wrinkles, and puffiness can add ten years to one's apparent age. After a sunbathing holiday, too, the eyes are apt to look anything but their best owing to the glare of sun on sea.

Three things are essential if you would keep your eyes young and beautiful. They must be cleansed, exercised, and rested daily. The lids must be waxen-smooth, and the delicate skin about them supple, firm, and free from crowsfeet.

Daily Cleansing

BATHE your eyes last thing at night and first thing every morning to remove every little particle of dust from under the lids, and to tone up the muscles.

A mild lotion is best for this purpose, and should be used in an eye-cup. Incline the head slightly, and hold the cup to each eye in turn, tilting the head backwards, and opening and closing the eyelid in it until the eye is thoroughly cleansed.

Hot salt-water compresses are an effective remedy for tired eyes. They help to relax the tense nerves and stimulate circulation, thus removing the tired, drawn appearance from round the eyes.

Dissolve one teaspoonful of ordinary table salt in half a tumblerful of very warm water. Wring out a large pad of cotton wool in salt water, and apply it to the closed eyes, replacing it as it cools with a fresh, hot compress.

Fifteen to twenty applications, taken while lying down in a darkened room, and followed by the application of a nourishing cream, will rejuvenate weary eyes.

Put on the cream generously round the eyes, working in lightly with the finger-tips, beginning at the bridge of the nose and gently drawing the finger-tips outwards over the upper lid and back under the eyes towards the starting point.

A refreshing treatment for tired eyes is to saturate pads of white lint in witch hazel or boracic lotion. Apply these to the eyes, which should be closed, and allow them to remain on the closed lids for ten minutes. This will help to remove signs of weariness or strain.

Exercises, Too

HERE are two exercises which will help you to keep your eyes young. The first simply consists of rolling the eyes. Open the lids as widely as possible and rotate the eyeballs rapidly— ten times to the right, ten times to the left.

Next, look straight ahead, keeping the lids wide apart until the eyes tingle. Close the lids and count slowly to ten. Open them, and repeat the exercise five times.

The next exercise should not be done more than twice in one day. Hold the right arm straight out in front of you, keeping the forefinger in a direct line with the nose. Move the finger slowly towards the nose, keeping the eyes focussed on it until the finger is within five inches from the tip of the nose, then slowly withdraw the finger until the hand is in its first position.

Close the eyes and count slowly to twenty, then repeat the exercise once more.

Day-time Make-Up

SOME women do not need daytime make-up for the eyes, but others whose brows and lashes are of a non-descript colouring are improved out of all knowledge by a little discreet make-up.

An indelible colouring may be used on eyebrows and lashes, and a touch of eye-shadow smoothed lightly over the upper lid will intensify the colour of the eyes, enhancing their beauty.

Make your Bathroom your Beauty Parlour

THIS dressing-table is built for the bathroom beauty parlour. In sea-green cellulose, it has a special mirror with damp-proof backing.

THE fastidious woman, whenever circumstance allows, will find it a great joy to have her beauty "work-table" in her bathroom, keeping on her bedroom toilet table merely her perfume spray and decorative brushes and comb. If she is living, after the modern fashion, in a one-room-and-bath flatlet, she can dispense with a dressing-table altogether in the bed-sitting-room.

Labour Saving

Nearly always the light in the bathroom is good, water is at hand, and there is no risk of spoiling carpets or dainty covers with powder and spilled lotions.

If it is not practicable to keep one's beauty things in the bathroom, it is a good idea to have a fitted-up bag, that can be carried from bedroom to bathroom, to contain all that is necessary to facial grooming.

Toilet bags with lightning fasteners are shaped like ordinary andbags, and contain face towel, tissues, two pots for cleansing and massage creams, and two bottles for lotions.

For Travelling

Baths, basins, towels, tooth-brushes, and face gloves have long since "gone gay," and now sponges can be had in orchid-mauve, buttercup-yellow, powder-blue, and flesh-pink.

Newcomers are capsules of pine needle salts (break one into your bath and you will imagine you are lying in a pine forest on a summer's day!); a romantic bath essence with dusting powder to match; cottonwool containers in pastel enamels, or a grander chromium affair for face tissues, meant to fix on the wall.

Or what about soap, shaped like a pineapple, which divides into sections and is perfumed with orange and citron? Or a telescopic back puff which packs into a small box, and is indispensable in these days of the backless gown?

Any of these things might well be an essential part of the modern woman's bathroom equipment all the year round.

Lifestyle

When not cooking, dressing, putting on makeup, doing household tasks or holding down a job, how did women in the 1930s enjoy themselves? Here again, the Daily Mail was on hand to guide them. How to give a dinner party without a cook? Simple. Rather than look harassed and make her guests uncomfortable, choose a fool-proof menu which can be prepared well in advance, even if it is something basic like Irish stew and fruit salad. ("It doesn't matter if you're little maid-of-all-work *does* make a mistake and hand from the right side now and again," writes the author). How to dance a tango in the night-club? Here are all 10 movements of the Right-hand Promenade Turn. Thin-faced? A touch of rouge on the chin will make a long face look shorter. Throughout these pages, despite the growing independence of women, it is taken for granted that the woman's role is to find a husband and then to please him, by preparing his meals, doing the housework and looking radiant when he comes home. In an article called Sweeping and Dusting Your Way to Beauty, a busy housewife complains that she has no time for slimming exercises. "But the very tasks of which they complain can, if done rhythmically and with the correct poise of the body, maintain just that slimness and grace which every woman desires," explains the author triumphantly. "Housework exercises are now taught in a London school where women learn rhythm in everyday tasks!". The Modern Age may have dawned in the 1930s, but it still had a very long way to go.

WEEK-END OUTFIT
You Can PACK *in a* SUITCASE.

Week-end party invitations, now that Spring is well on the way, are beginning to pour in. Here Odette has planned an outfit which can be adapted for brief visits to country cottages or flying expeditions to Paris.

A WEEK-END outfit varies according to the kind of week-end involved.

There is the week-end for which one feels one has been invited purely and simply to weed the garden, and there is the week-end during which one is rushed round to all the excitements—urban and rural—within a sixty-miles radius. There is also the week-end trip to Paris.

The latter two are likely to be something of a strain on a suitcase wardrobe unless the greatest discrimination is used in the choice of garments.

Ubiquitous "Four Piece."

The new interpretation of the four-piece ensemble—a top coat, jacket, skirt and blouse—furnishes the basis of the outfit in either case. The first three items may match exactly or be of different materials that "compose" successfully.

For the ordinary week-end in a country house I would suggest a tweed top coat in a mixture of colouring that gives a pastel effect, a checked skirt that shows up the same colours more definitely, and a cardigan coat—of the new type, with four pockets and a belt, as shown at the extreme left of the sketch—of either flannel or suède tricot in one of the brighter colours of the tweed.

This cardigan may be plain, or bordered with narrow bands of the skirt material as shown in the sketch. A silk shirt worn with a tie or large bow, a felt hat in a pastel shade to match the overcoat, loose chamois gloves, and brown calf shoes, with thick silk or cashmere stockings, complete the ensemble.

What to Pack.

All these things will be worn for the journey, whether by road or rail, leaving the suitcase accommodation free for underclothing and night attire, a spare shirt or thin woollen jumper, a simple crêpe day dress, an evening dress of printed chiffon or lace that can be packed into a small space without showing creases, heavy shoes for golf or walking, satin shoes for the evening, a beret or tricot cap, and a compact array of toilet requisites.

It is taken for granted that underclothing of the most modern type is chosen—silk tricot combinations with woven brassière tops, instead of yesterday's cami-knickers, tailored knickers that dispense with every vestige of superfluous fullness, and an unlined dressing-gown of printed silk and on severely masculine lines.

In the Sketch.

The sketch shows two excellent top coats (on the 2nd and 4th figures from the left). Both have loose armholes that enable them to be worn over another jacket quite comfortably. The latter has the short scarf collar that is having a great success in Paris, and is trimmed with lines of stitching; the former has the fullness at the waistline disposed of by tucks and an *inserted* belt.

On this figure is shown, too, one of the most effective of the new tweed and felt hats for motoring. The tweed "brim" is continued at either side into long scarf ends which are crossed in front and carried round to the back of the neck, where they are tied or knotted.

"Transformation" Tie.

Many of the new coats are made without collars of any kind, but are supplied with separate cravat ties.

The figure at the extreme right shows an outfit that would form the mainstay of a similar wardrobe intended for Paris.

A dark bluish tweed is chosen for the costume and beige washing satin for the tunic. A beige felt hat and beige gloves are important items of the ensemble. Two cravat ties, one in the tweed and one in beige satin, should be included in this wardrobe. The tweed one could be worn with a tuck-in shirt and blue felt hat for travelling and morning wear, the satin one with the matching tunic for afternoons.

Accessories That Are Chic.

Among the chic accessories to the week-end outfit shown in the sketch are a tweed bag with a deep mount of inlaid wood in different colours to match those appearing in the tweed, a large bunch of field flowers, and a string of carved wooden beads.   ODETTE.

Lady Campbell writes

Sir Malcolm's Article—and Declares

Women Drivers are Better than Men!

It is time justice was handed to the mere woman who drives her own car—Lady Campbell at the wheel.

S IR Malcolm Campbell, the Motoring Editor of "The Daily Mail," is on his way home from Miami, Florida, where last week he set up a new world's land speed record so Lady Campbell takes his place with a racy defence of the woman motorist.

This article is the first of a short series which Lady Campbell will contribute to "The Daily Mail."

◆◆◆◆◆◆◆◆◆◆◆◆◆◆◆◆◆◆◆◆◆◆◆◆◆◆◆◆◆

A S a regular reader of motoring articles, I have been forced to the conclusion that we women are not popular among the opposite sex, at least as drivers of motor-cars.

We Drive Better

Really it is time a little justice was handed out to the mere woman who has the audacity to insist upon driving her own car—and, on the average, does it better. Yes, Mr. Man, women *are* better drivers than men.

Let us examine the alleged offences to which we women are said to be prone.

To begin with, we know nothing about the amenities of the road and are utterly lacking in " road sense."

Fewer Accidents

If that means a knowledge of road usage which enables us to drive without being a menace to others and to keep clear of accident, then I say we *do* possess it, and in ever greater measure than does the male driver. Proportionately to numbers, we women drivers figure better in the accident statistics than do men.

Another charge levelled against us is that we have no mechanical sense and are rough on our cars. Once again I join issue with the attackers.

In these days of comparative mechanical perfection of the car, when every operation, including that of gear changing, has ceased to be a matter of brute force, the lighter, defter touch of the woman gives her an advantage just where she is said to be lacking.

The Gear-Crashers

Where the woman driver does score is that she is subconsciously aware of her shortcomings in this direction and therefore refrains from taking chances which the man, conscious of his superior judgment, will accept—and often find out that he is wrong.

Again, we are said to know nothing about the mechanical side of our cars. We have not, generally speaking, the remotest idea of what it is that makes the wheels go round.

I am not going to contend that every woman motorist is an accomplished mechanic, for I do know that quite a number of very competent drivers are abysmally ignorant of everything that concerns the mechanics of the motor-car, but is not the same true of men? Of course it is; and again taking the average, I am perfectly certain that

we women do not lag behind our menfolk in our mechanical knowledge of the car.

There is a little something the men forget when they accuse us of this want of knowledge. I suppose I ought not to give away my sex, but the opportunity is too tempting.

I believe the West African natives will tell you that the monkey is a very clever little person. He could talk if he wanted, but he knows that, if he did, man would at once put him to work—so he doesn't !

And, speaking now as Mrs. Everywoman, I certainly am not going to jack up my own car on a muddy road to change a wheel, or to do a dirty job under the bonnet, when I can by an assumption of helpless ignorance get it done for me by a large, hefty man who is simply bubbling over with superiority.

It Saves Trouble

Then there is the question of whether women should take part in motor racing or not.

Women have proved that they are quite as capable of driving racing cars at high speed as men. The most important race at Brooklands during the year just past was won by two women driving as a team.

Just Jealousy !

I suspect that the opposition is simply due to jealousy. In the days when racing was confined to the male animal, he who drove fast cars was an idol, adored by the whole flapper tribe. Once, however, woman invaded his sphere and showed that she could more than hold her own, much of the glamour disappeared and the motor-racing male ceased to be a hero to his gallery.

Naturally he simply hated it. Hence his efforts to keep us out.

I have no wish to race again, but I am all on the side of the woman who does, because I know that on the track, as on the road, the woman driver is equal to, if not better than, the man.

"WHAT SHALL I GIVE THEM?"

Our Shop "Detective" helps you to make out your Christmas present list—from the very latest novelties.

For Mother—
who likes entertaining

COCKTAIL set in red and gold lacquered glass, on a tray large enough to hold the olives and other appetisers—easy to hand round.

A beautiful handbag in parchment leather, hand-embroidered in Chinese design.

Condiment set in pastel coloured Poole pottery.

Bow in diamanté, to be worn on the hair, dress, or hat—yet another Edwardian revival.

Necklace of wood and steel in Empire design—a successful combination of old and new.

Cushion in glazed and quilted chintz—charming for a country house.

❖ ❖ ❖

For Father—
who enjoys a week-end's shooting

All - weather woolly jerkin which "zips" right up to the throat—designed by a famous shot.

Sheepskin overshoes for the long drive home

Waterproof "holdalot" to carry sleeping kit. Has a "zip" fastener and will stand any amount of cramming.

Wallet in leathers of various prices. Has a special attachment to defeat the pickpocket.

Book of entertaining after-dinner stories.

❖ ❖ ❖

For the Son—
who is a bachelor car-owner

ELECTRIC lamp on rubber suction pad, to be attached to any part of the car. Can be used for inspection, parking light, or emergency tail-lamp.

A flexible, expanding luggage brace—saves all that strapping and is safe and strong.

Cap and scarf set in checked tweed, warm and smart.

Dressing-gown in the new woven stripe flannel, with plain self-coloured collar and cuffs.

Electric plate-warmer for the bachelor flat.

❖ ❖ ❖

For the Daughter—
who appreciates a touch of chic

SET of bracelets in three tones —brown, amber, and flesh, or black, smoke-grey, and white. New enough for the ultra-smart.

Square enamel powder case that slides open at a touch.

A Tudor head-dress in unbreakable crystal and diamanté.

Belt in green python skin with steel hooks and clasp.

Fitted leather case with lotion bottle, powder box, lipstick, cigarette case, and lighter in black and silver; has a compartment to hold pyjamas and is an ideal "one-night" bag.

Sequin necklace and bracelet of gold on silver. Also a circular clip in pale green mirror glass and diamanté.

❖ ❖ ❖

For the Children—
who have all the modern ideas

Modern doll's house furniture, including kitchen cabinets, carpet-sweepers, leather arm-chairs, chromium-fitted baths, and wardrobe trunks.

Adorable lion cubs, sturdy cart-horses, and Negro and Mexican dolls in gay suits. Models of famous racing cars.

Aeroplane parts for the young mechanic to assemble. Electric speedway for dirt-track racing.

Telephone which can be wired from room to room.

Baby doll which arrives in an attaché case, complete with clothes, rattle, powder-puff, and sponge. A training in efficient nursery methods !

❖ ❖ ❖

For Aunt—
who lives " on her own "

Hand-woven travelling rug in featherweight Galloway tweed —lovely warm colours.

For more domestic moments— proofed satin apron and cooking sleeves in rose or blue.

Evening cape in chené taffeta, in blue or lavender shades.

❖ ❖ ❖

For Uncle—
who is a convivial soul

Hunting horn table lighter which gives a flame when picked up.

Cabinet of conjuring tricks, to make a success of his Christmas party.

Heavy ashtray of green glass —very large, practical, and inexpensive.

❖ ❖ ❖

For Granny—
who likes something useful

Sets of tray-cloths made to fit the tea-trolley—two cloths with four napkins to match.

Miniature carpet - sweeper, which can be used from a chair.

❖ ❖ ❖

For the Dog—
who must have a present, too

Dandy brush and comb in a gay leather case, or a drinking bowl with his portrait painted on it.

OSTRICH feathers have been used to make most alluring necklaces. The sketch shows an example in melon pink, entwined with pearls and fastened with a massive crystal clasp at the centre back—another attractive present for an elegant woman.

WOMAN at the WHEEL

We Like Pretty Cars— but they must be Practical

By Lady (Malcolm) Campbell

Lady Campbell studies car comfort.

WHETHER it is that I failed to find the winner of the Derby, or that none of my Irish Sweep tickets drew even a modest £100 I do not know, but I am certainly full of complaints this week.

I have been reading through the R.A.C. regulations for the conduct of Concours d'Elegance. Of course, one has to agree that these events do not entirely appeal to the woman competitor. Their clear intention is to assist in improving the breed of the motor-car, with particular attention paid to the coach-work part of the vehicle. That is excellent: but I cannot help thinking that if the R.A.C. and the trade bodies which consult with the club on these matters had asked two or three practical women motorists for their assistance the rules might have been slightly different.

* * *

MY main objection is that far too many marks are allotted for "beauty." I confess it is a joy to me to regard a beautiful motor-car, but it is a case in which beauty can be said to be only skin deep!

* * *

THERE are such considerations as comfort, convenience, ease of control, visibility of the road from the driving seat, lightness of steering,

and a dozen other points which are of the first importance to the woman who drives and looks after her own car.

I know a car—it must be nameless: it is not the only offender—which would take first prize in any competition judged on beauty of line only.

The model I mean is known as a close-coupled coupé and is as pretty as a picture. It is of the two-door type, and the doors, which are very wide, open rearwards. They are heavy, as these wide doors must be, and, if you happen to stop on a road which has a sideways slope and you want to open the door against it the physical effort needed is quite considerable.

* * *

I HAVE known doors, too, to fly open while driving. If it should happen in this case you are lucky indeed if the only damage is a pair of badly wrenched hinges. I admit that the two-door saloon, or close coupé, has its merits, but in competition I should deduct marks for such doors.

* * *

THIS same car has the change-speed lever so placed that you have to reach for it at the risk of braining yourself against the dash. You can, I believe, buy as an extra a "remote control" arrangement to make this more accessible, but the very fact is eloquent of want of thought.

You cannot, when you are in the driving seat, see anything on the near side of the radiator cap, so low is the seat pitched for beauty of outline.

I am quite sure that these low-pitched cars are entirely responsible for what is known as kerb-shyness. You think you are driving within a few inches of the edge of the road when, in fact, you are three feet away.

* * *

DOOR - HANDLES that get caught up in your sleeve or in your driving gauntlets are another abomination—and they are so unnecessary. Doors that rattle and windows that stick in their guides and refuse to wind either up or down are another of my grumbles for a thoroughly discontented week. Do, please Mr. Motor Manufacturer, cease this quest for beauty and give more attention to the points I have noted in my opening as being even more desirable than appear-

ances to the practically minded woman of the car.

I know you have done a great deal for us and are willing to do more, but don't, I beg of you, be led away by those who tell you that all we care about are good looks in the car of our choice.

* * *

I CAME across, the other day, a neat little accessory for the woman motorist who enjoys a cigarette at the wheel. This is a natty leather cigarette case, with a compartment to hold matches, which clips on the steering wheel so that one's attention is not distracted while fumbling for cigarettes and matches in the bad old way. I confess to a liking for a smoke while driving, and I find this new case quite a boon.

Another useful item I have discovered is a belt which has a round zip-fastened purse attached to it. You know what a nuisance it is to have to search through your handbag for money to pay when filling up or anything of the kind. This way of carrying your loose change saves quite a lot of time and temper.

* * *

IF you are planning a motoring holiday, let me urge you to see that the car is in the pink of condition before you start. It is so much better to anticipate trouble and remove the possible source before you start than to have your holiday spoilt by untoward happenings for which there is no earthly excuse.

Quite probably your engine has not been decarbonised since last season. Have it done now, and the valves properly ground in. Then, the oil should be changed in engine, gear-box and back axle, and the car thoroughly greased all round.

* * *

THAT you are not likely to be using the lights much now is no reason for neglecting the battery. The starter imposes a considerable drain upon it, and in most modern cars the ignition system depends upon the battery. Make up the acid level with distilled water, clean the terminals and give them a good thick coating of vaseline.

This Schiaparelli suit of rough brown linen has a belt-purse which is useful for the woman driver.

SANTOS CASANI

Offers Some Hints for

COOL DANCING

ONE of the greatest mistakes that can be made by the man dancer in search of coolness is to wear shoes with very thin soles and fine silk socks.

The foot action in ballroom dancing is a glide, so that the feet are in almost continuous contact with the floor, and a little thought will make it clear that the friction set up and the heat consequently generated is greater than in walking. Therefore the more the feet are insulated the better.

I am not, of course, suggesting that the dancer should wear hiking boots, but he will find that a lisle sock or one of fine wool in a shoe with a light walking sole will be infinitely more comfortable in hot weather than any thinner footwear.

Stick To Stockings

I am not going to advise women against wearing silk stockings, but I must warn them emphatically against dancing *without* stockings.

That again looks and sounds much cooler than it will be found in practice.

Moreover, it will almost certainly result in blistered heels, especially in the case of women who do not dance habitually.

Another mistake commonly made by dancers is in the matter of " cooling-off."

Going from a warm dancing-room to a much cooler place may be temporarily very refreshing, but the effect will not last.

Reducing your temperature below that of the room in which you are going to dance will only make you feel warmer when you return.

For the same reason it is a mistake to attempt to keep cool by standing in the direct breeze of a fan.

Fans in the dance hall should be arranged so that their breezes do not play directly on the dancers. Their purpose is to renew the air in the room as often as possible and with the minimum of disturbance.

Much the same applies to drinks. Hot tea or coffee will be found more refreshing in the long run than ice-water.

And all these things are matters of health as well as comfort. Neglect of this advice is the most common cause of the summer cold.

Next week I shall give some useful hints on lawn or grass dancing, a subject about which I am asked a host of questions every summer.

Now to proceed with the lessons on variations: We continue with the Tango, and the next step is the Right-hand Promenade Turn.

THE TANGO—
—The Right-hand Promenade Turn

THE peculiarity of this variation is that, unlike other turns, all of which you start walking forward, it begins and finishes sideways and in line of dance.

This step, which should follow a Promenade, is done in ten movements

and takes up three and a half bars of the music, which is fourteen beats.

The best way to start is feet together, with the balance on the right foot. From this position—

(1) Step sideways and in line of dance with the left foot; bring the weight on to the left foot. (Slow, two beats.)

(2) Turning slightly to the right, step sideways and in line of dance with the right foot, crossing it over the left; bring the weight on to the right foot, the right toe being pointed outwards. (Quick, one beat.)

(3) Turning slightly more to the right, take a short step backwards and in line of dance with the left foot; bring the weight on to the left foot. **(See Fig. A.)** (Quick, one beat.)

(4) Step straight back and in line of dance with the right foot; bring the weight on to the right foot **(Fig. B).** (Slow, two beats.)

(5) Continuing the turn to the right, step back with the left foot; bring the weight on to the left foot, the left toe being turned inwards **(Fig. C).** (Quick, one beat.)

(6) Turning further to the right, take a short step forwards and in line of dance with the right foot; bring the weight on to the right foot, the toe of which should be turned slightly out. (Quick, one beat.)

(7) Turning slightly more to the right, step sideways and in line of dance with the left foot; bring the weight on to the left foot. (Slow, two beats.)

(8) Step sideways and in line of dance with the right foot, crossing it over the left; bring the weight on to the right foot. (Quick, one beat.)

(9) Step sideways and in line of dance with the left foot; bring the weight on to the left foot **(Fig. D).** (Quick, one beat.)

(10) Close the right foot to the left foot; bring the weight on to the right foot. (Slow, two beats.)

From this position, with the left foot, which should be disengaged, you can do an ordinary Promenade, a Double Promenade (explained last week), the Link-step (explained in an earlier lesson), or this Right-hand Promenade Turn again.

These are the man's steps. The woman's are the reverse, with the exception that in movements (4) and (5) she goes outside her partner and in the remaining movements she is brought back into her original position.

To learn this step it is advisable to practise it with a partner.

* * *

Mr. Santos Casani invites readers who want advice to write to him c/o *The Daily Mail*, Northcliffe House, E.C. 4, enclosing a stamped addressed envelope. Back numbers containing former lessons can be had at 2d. a copy from the *Daily Mail* Back Number Dept., 130, Fleet-street, E.C. 4.

Right

Wrong

Right—and Wrong

THESE two pictures show the correct (above) and the wrong (right) hold in dancing. Stand with your partner in front of a mirror and compare the reflection with the illustration, noticing particularly these points:—
1. Exact position of the arms, which gives correct alignment.
2. The way the man's arm is placed

round his partner, in the only position in which it can convey correct indications.
3. The position of the man's right hand on the woman's back, with the fingers closed.
4. The linking of the man's left hand with the woman's right.
5. The position and angle of the elbows, which help tremendously in deportment and balance.

6. The position of the heads. If this is wrong the view of both dancers is obstructed: the man cannot guide properly and the woman cannot see to warn him of impending collisions.

A Letter to...

HOLIDAY GIRLS

from...

THOMAS COLUMB

BANK Holiday! This day of days when thousands of oh, so modern women disport themselves by land and sea! Off you go to enjoy yourselves with never a care or thought in the world . . . and that is just what I am afraid of.

Now I, as a bachelor and an observer of that life in the raw that is so very seldom mild, intend to give you, whether you like it or not, my view of some of the things you should do, and some of the things you should avoid, to heighten the charm and increase the prestige of your astonishing sex.

Many of you, of course, will patronise one of those long, low, and incredibly fast cars, piloted by the lucky man of your choice.

Then do I beseech you to sit there demurely by his side wearing a rapturous expression, just gazing from time to time at him with an adoring look. For then he will reflect that never has he taken out a girl who has shown so much intelligence and understanding. Then is the scalp yours and the poor fish hooked.

But here my heart misgives me, for I know the way otherwise slow girls behave in fast cars.

They get all "het up." They screech and yell with laughter. They sprawl all over the machine. They clutch their driver's elbow as he is turning a peculiarly congested corner. They are, in fact a menace to the life of the populace and frighten away young men from matrimony. And you river girls! How attractive you can look as you lie with easy grace in a punt clad in a delicious white, cool-looking frock, appearing so devastatingly helpless!

But the moment you take to punting yourself, the while you utter hoarse noises as you whirl the punt round in circles, your charm is gone. You become a blot on the flowing stream.

Unforgivable!

Remember, I beseech you, that every young man who takes a pretty girl for an outing on the river is convinced he can punt.

To take the law literally into your own hands wreaks havoc with a young man's self esteem. For this he will never forgive you.

Good heavens, punts are especially put on the water for girls to look girlish and wayward in.

And sea bathing!

I recall one fine day . . . here is a very sad tale in a very sad life . . . taking out a damsel with me to the sea to bathe. She was charming . . . she was fair to behold . . but not in her bathing dress.

She tripped down to the sea with her hair dragged back from her head, wearing a bathing suit of bright purple She looked awful. She seared my eyes She made me catch the first train home.

You really must try to look your best even in the sea. Remember that your companion wants to think of you as a mermaid and not as a floating scarecrow.

Take pains with the sea. It will repay you. Cast your bread carefully upon the waters and it will return to you in an hour or less.

Now another sad tale When I was a young flying officer training to fly in the war I prevailed on my squadron commander to allow me to take up a friend of mine for a flight.

He refused. He then looked at my friend. He consented.

All went well till we were about five hundred feet up in the air. Suddenly without any warning, for she was sitting behind me, my passenger let out an appalling yell.

" Let me out." she screamed. " Let me out! "

With this she stood up and entwined her arms round my neck bellowing like an elephant.

Aeroplanes in those days had to be treated with respect. So had their pilots. With the greatest difficulty I managed to land the machine.

Then for five minutes I told my passenger exactly what I thought of her. No wedding bells rang Should the man of your choice be an airman and such a half-wit as to consent to give you a flight, just gaze at the back of his neck and say and do nothing. Then when you land love may bloom.

Longs and Shorts

Now what of hiking, that very modern frivolity and exercise with the dreadful name? Should you desire to venture forth with some cheery companions on a walking expedition, by all means wear shorts. But only, I implore you, if you are slim and of a pleasing shape.

Should the hand of Nature have slipped when delineating your contours, do not for mercy's sake attempt such a costume.

For to the discerning masculine eye there are few sights more shattering or more romance-killing than the sight of a girl who should never wear shorts but invariably does. Which is the long and short of it.

And so I might go on For I wish you all so very well on this holiday of yours, and I should be so sorry if by any thoughtless word or deed you fell in the estimation of anyone for whom you cared

For it is the little things that count in life's holidays, which may be trite, I own, but is so terrifyingly apt on this particular Monday.

A WOMAN'S HOUSEHOLD DIARY.

Seven Attic Suggestions at Next Week's Great Exhibition.

UNUSUALLY low furniture, specially designed by a London firm to suit an attic room is a feature of the " Room in the Roof " section at the *Daily Mail* Ideal Home Exhibition, which will open at Olympia on Monday.

The typically untidy attic, with small window and dingy wallpaper, is exactly the same size and shape as the half-dozen other rooms which an architect has converted into attractive living-rooms.

All seven rooms measure 14ft. 9in. by 12ft., the ceiling sloping from 8ft. to 5ft. high.

* * *

To Show What You Can Do.

One is a boy's workshop, papered in silver to give a metallic impression, and fitted with carpentering tables, benches, and a model train and station. A girl's bedroom is decorated in soft greys and green, while a bachelor's flat is made from an attic divided into two small rooms—bedroom and smoking lounge. The lighting is concealed behind panels of glass in the ceiling.

The divan in the girl's bedroom has a separate bed-head, which can be detached during the day, and acts both as a table and perfumery cupboard. A little chest of six drawers measures only 2ft. 6in. in height.

* * *

Cheap—but Effective.

At the Kingsway Theatre première of " The Artist and the Shadow " the other evening I liked the decorative effect of the hangings in the artist's Paris studio. Clear lacquer-red curtains, a piece of checked red, green and blue fabric hanging on a banister-rail, and a Paisley shawl used as a divan-cover were cheap and effective suggestions for brightening a living room.

Un fortunately, the artist grows rich, and by the third act the studio has curtains of blue velvet and silver brocade, and depressingly prosperous-looking Chinese bric-à-brac disposed here and there.

* * *

Fish on Lenten Menus.

Fish displays are featured at several London provision stores this week, and I found the fish counters thronged with women when I was shopping the other morning. The Lent season, and the growing realisation of the food value of fish—explained by Sir Arbuthnot Lane in this page recently—are greatly stimulating the demand.

Fresh salmon from the fisheries of Scotland and Ireland is being sold for 4s. a pound in a Brompton-road store, and among the less expensive varieties cod, at 1s. a pound, is most popular. An attractive selection of preserved fish for salads is being offered at special Lent prices.

* * *

To-day's Recipe.—Baked Curry.

Cut some meat into dice, and for two cupfuls allow an equal quantity of chopped apple and celery mixed, a tea-spoonful of curry powder, a cup of uncooked rice and four cupfuls of milk.

Mix all together and put into a greased fireproof dish. Bake slowly for an hour and a half.

* * *

For Soiled Hands.

Spring cleaning, investigating the engine of one's car, gardening, and other jobs one usually undertakes just now are apt to make the hands incredibly dirty, and some sort of cleanser should be put in every bathroom. A woman owner of a private printing press has just tested a new preparation which, she finds, removes printer's ink even after the very messy work of breaking up type. It is simply rubbed on the hands before washing, is London made, and costs 1s. 3d. the tube.

THIS new electric stove, enamelled in blue and white, will arouse much interest at the *Daily Mail* Ideal Home Exhibition next week. The oven is enamelled throughout, a hot cupboard is fitted below the oven, and the boiling plate by the side takes square pots as shown.

Minor Points that Make for Chic.

FUR is used lavishly for evening coats, both of the ankle-length and thigh-length variety. The first sketch shows a model in black velvet edged with white fox; the second a thigh-length coat in gold brocade edged with black fox, the fan-shaped collar being typical of the mode.

Thousands Spent in Fur Trimming.

Thousands of pounds' worth of fur—red, silver, white, blue and dyed fox, lynx, ermine, monkey—have been used by Norman Hartnell *for the trimmings alone* in his summer collection of day and evening models. This designer's theory is that fur enhances the beauty of most women, and for coats has the definitely practical purpose of weighing down the hem when the fabric is light and summery.

SKATING *Improves* the Figure

NOW that the ice-rinks are open for the winter, why not take up skating as an easy way to attain the fashionable figure?

During the summer I added 8lb. to my weight. But I know from past experience that I shall banish these extra pounds during the winter, while I am skating every day. Since I first took up skating five years ago I have become not only fitter but much slimmer.

Graceful Outline

I do not recommend skating merely to reduce the weight. The special point of skating as an exercise is that it produces that slender, yet gracefully developed outline which is demanded by the new directoire gowns which are being shown at the important dress houses just now.

It is round the waist that the skater grows slimmer. Every skating movement tends to this result, and as you skate the flesh is actually massaged away between hips and ribs as in professionally taught exercises.

This in itself gives a more shapely figure. In addition, skating teaches deportment, producing a graceful carriage.

Answers to Correspondents

The Daily Mail's Women's Bureau had so many letters that Victoria Chappelle, Joan Beringer and the other experts had their work cut out to answer them. Human nature was no different 70 years ago. Young women were anxious about their complexions, mothers were anxious about their children, housewives wanted to know what to do with a tin of shrimps, or soup that had come out too salty (answer, add a few slices of raw potato and cook a bit longer). Children's diets in fact were much better than today's. Asked what to bring for school lunches, Sister Cooper SRN recommends brown bread sandwiches filled with chopped banana, or grated cheese or raw carrot, honey or egg and cress. Less healthy, in retrospect, was her advice to check children's shoe size in a high street X-ray machine - something older readers will remember. Women wrote in about sagging face muscles (wear a chin-strap) and bosom development (try deep breathing). SYZ in Chelsea, needing to bleach away a tan, is told to slice off a piece of cucumber and rub it round her neck, leave it to dry and then massage with cold cream. "My knuckles are thick. How can I get them slimmer. I am only 26," asks another woman plaintively. See a doctor: you may be rheumatic, advises Joan Beringer - "meanwhile steep the fingers in a solution of warm water and Epsom Salts." How do I prevent bed springs from creaking? asks Mrs H from Bangor. Increase the tension, comes back the answer. As if we didn't know.

HOUSEWIFERY—Jennifer Snow

SUGGEST curtains for tiny dining room facing north but with very high ceiling and high placed windows.
Thorpeness. H.A.M.

Have a cream ground striped with primrose and orange. The cream of the ceiling should be brought down over the cornice as far as the picture rail, to meet the primrose of the walls and so reduce the height of the room.

COOKERY—Doris B. Sheridan

CAN you tell me how to make a sweetmeat called Pistachio Nougat?
Wimbledon, S.W. (MRS.) S. J.

Put together into a saucepan 3 egg whites, 1lb. sieved icing sugar, 1 tablespoonful vanilla and ½lb. clear honey and stir over slow heat for twenty minutes. Add 1 tablespoonful whole pistachio nuts, 2 tablespoonfuls roughly chopped almonds and 2oz. cut up glacé cherries. Pack the mixture into a Neapolitan ice box, which has been lined with wafer paper, place a piece of wafer paper on top and, when set, cut into bars.

CHILDREN AND THE NURSERY
—Sister Cooper, S.R.N.

AMOUNT of sleep required at 9 months.
Worcester. (MRS.) B.

Baby should sleep about 16 hours out of the 24 at this age. Probably two hours in the morning, and only half an hour in the afternoon.

MY seventeen-months old daughter takes solid food well, particularly potato and bread and butter, but only drinks about 8 ounces in the day.
Newport, I.O.W. (MRS.) S.

Withhold the solids for a time, always starting the meals with a drink. She seems to have an excess of starchy food at present, which is unwise, though potato is satisfactory.

DRESS—Victoria Chappelle

WHAT accessories should I wear with a tailored coat in black and white pin-stripe suiting?
New Southgate. RENE.

The colour of hat depends on colour of frock you will wear beneath the coat. If it is black or black and white, you might wear a black or white hat, or one in coral, cherry, clear red, or clear green. With a coloured frock wear one to match it or a black one. Choose black shoes, beige stockings and gloves.

BEAUTY—Joan Beringer

WHAT colour to suit pale complexion? Should I use rouge?
Hounslow. (MRS.) R. Q.

I should use a powder in a light apricot shade to give warmth to your skin. Certainly use a little rouge. Choose one with a hint of orange in it.

COOKERY—Doris B. Sheridan

RECIPE for Toffee Apples.
Edinburgh. (MRS.) HALLAM.

Wash about 14 good sized apples and put on sticks. Put in saucepan 1lb. yellow crystals sugar, 6 tablespoonfuls water, and ¼ teaspoonful cream of tartar, and stil until sugar melts and boils. Boil hard without stirring for 8 minutes, and test by dipping a wooden skewer in cold water, in toffee and in cold water again. If toffee is brittle it is ready. Plunge in the apples and turn them into greased tins till set.

BEAUTY—Joan Beringer

MY fair hair gets greasy quickly, and seems to be darkening. How can I prevent this?
Calne. J. K.

Get two camomile shampoos for your hair. Mix a portion of these together into a paste with a little warm water; apply paste to the roots of the hair, and leave on for ten minutes before washing it. Wash with the rest of the shampoo in the ordinary way. Give your scalp daily massage with a tonic and when washing the hair, while it is still quite wet after the final rinse, rub some eau-de-Cologne well into the scalp.

DRESS—Victoria Chappelle

I HAVE quite a good knee-length coat of fine black pony-skin, but the sleeves are much worn. I cannot afford to have new fur.
London. EARNEST.

Put in sleeves of thick black cloth made a little full just below the shoulders and then slim and fitting. A wide belt of matching cloth can be added.

COOKERY—Doris B. Sheridan

HOW to make blackberry jelly set; it is merely thick syrup.
Sunderland. M. R.

Add gelatine in the proportion of about an ounce to a pint of liquid. The quantity must be governed by the texture of the syrup. Remember that preserves set in this way do not keep indefinitely.

CHILDREN AND THE NURSERY—
Sister Cooper, S.R.N.

CORRECT temperature for a young baby's bath.
Halifax. (MRS.) H.

100 deg. Fahrenheit is correct. This should be tested with a bath thermometer, or should feel just warm to your elbow.

BEAUTY—Joan Beringer

I HAVE to wear glasses. Do you advise ones with rims or the rimless kind? I am fair, with dark blue eyes.
Sheringham. LILY.

Have horn-rimmed glasses; large ones, unless your face is very small. Choose ones with blonde tortoiseshell or imitation tortoiseshell rims.

DRESS—Victoria Chappelle

WHAT colour can I wear with a brown evening gown?
Birmingham. (MRS.) S. LINTON.

A faded turquoise blue, or a dusty pink looks well with brown.

HOUSEWIFERY—Jennifer Snow

WOULD you kindly suggest an outside colour scheme for my bungalow?
Llanfairfechan. GIMROE.

Have the main body of the building in creamy white, broken with black for windows and doors. A red roof fits into both summer and winter landscapes.

COOKERY—Doris B. Sheridan

HOW to make sherry sauce to serve with Christmas pudding.
Motherwell. (MRS.) F. M.

Put the yolks of two eggs, ½ wineglassful each of sherry and water, and ½ teaspoonful sugar into a saucepan. Stand the pan in a second pan of boiling water and whisk until the sauce is thick and frothy.

BEAUTY—Joan Beringer

HOW should one apply white of egg for wrinkles round the eyes?
Nottingham. F.

This is a strong astringent and should not be used too often. The white can be slightly beaten and painted round the eyes with a camel-hair brush when you want to give your face a quick cocktail. It should be left on until dry, and then removed with a pad of cotton wool moistened in warm water.

NURSERY—Sister Cooper, S.R.N.

HOW can I extract raw carrot juice?
Urm. MRS. R.

Dip a well-scrubbed carrot into boiling water for 10 seconds, then grate it —using one of the new straight graters —on to a boiled cheese cloth. Squeeze the cloth containing the grated pieces into a clean cup. Give to baby undiluted after the age of 7 months.

DRESS—Victoria Chappelle

SUGGEST how I can arrange a knee-length coat of a costume which is too tight across the front.
Brighton. WORRIED.

Cut away about eight inches each side of the front and insert long fronts and turn-overs collar of fur-cloth buttoning down on the edge. This front should stop about 6in. above the coat hem.

HOUSEWIFERY—Jennifer Snow

HOW to prevent bed springs from creaking.
Bangor. (MRS.) H.

If you have the springs tightened so that the mattress is extended to the fullest tension, you will prevent the springs jarring against one another, which is the cause of the noise.

BEAUTY—Joan Beringer

STYLE of hairdressing to make very thin face look fuller—dark hair—long bob.
London. ROBBEE.

Have the ends of your hair curled and your parting very low on one side; brush it well back from the ears and wear it in a bunch of curls at the back of the head. A pair of large stud earrings will add width to your face.

COOKERY—Doris B. Sheridan

A RECIPE for Royal Icing.
Harting. D. C. M.

Sieve 10oz. icing sugar and beat it gradually into the whites of four eggs. When the mixture is sufficiently stiff to hold its shape when dropped from the spoon beat in a dessertspoonful of lemon juice.

NURSERY—Sister Cooper, S.R.N.

PLEASE suggest a diet which may help to cure enlarged tonsils.
North Ferriby. (MRS.) R.

Cut down soft starches and sweets, especially white sugar. Give natural sugars in dried fruits, beetroot, and grapes. Starch should be given at one meal only, in the form of potato cooked in its skin, toasted wholemeal bread, or one of the many rye-breads now obtainable. Raw vegetables and fruit should be given daily.

DRESS—Victoria Chappelle

HOW can I disguise a thin back and shoulde s on a frock which in the pattern is rather deeply cut at the back?
Leamington Spa. F. R. T.

Have your frock made with the high front neck line slightly draped and insert in the back double silk net cut to give a deep cowl effect. This will disguise your back without taking away from the smartness of the dress.

HOUSEWIFERY—Jennifer Snow

TO remove damp from picture mount.
Staines. SUSSEX.

Make a weak solution of chloride of lime—about 1 teaspoonful to 1 quart of water (warm) and paint the stains over, drying them immediately with blotting paper and repeating the process. Do not saturate.

COOKERY—Doris B. Sheridan

HOW to make baked sponge pudding.
Rugby. (MISS) S.

Beat 4oz. each butter and sugar to a cream, adding the grated rind of a lemon, a well-whipped egg, and a little milk. Fold in lightly 4oz. self raising flour. Turn into a well-buttered mould and bake for about an hour in a fairly hot oven.

BEAUTY—Joan Beringer.

HOW can I check a tendency towards double chin?
Blackpool. BUZZ.

Exercise and the use of astringent lotion or cream will help to reduce the chin. Sharp patting, using the backs of the fingers, is a good massage to practise frequently during the day.

CHILDREN AND THE NURSERY
—Sister Cooper, S.R.N.

HOW can overweight be prevented when baby is naturally fed? I have noted your remarks about fat babies.
Thornton Heath. (MRS.) T.

Water before feeds and shorter feeds must be given. Many babies take all they need in 4 minutes. Exercise must be increased on the firm floor, and clothing adjusted. Food is fuel, and if the heat of the body is kept in too well all food taken goes to making weight.

HOUSEWIFERY—Jennifer Snow

HOW to season a cast iron frying pan.
Kidderminster. E. ANDREWS.

All frying pans require seasoning when new. Cover the bottom of the pan with coarse kitchen salt, and heat till the salt dissolours. Empty the pan, rub round with soft paper and repeat three times.

DRESS—Victoria Chappelle

SUGGEST edging for shoulder cape of black and white check light wool frock.
Hants. M. T. F.

I do not advise edging of any kind. The material is elaborate enough. But a strip of the same check might be used to finish off.

BEAUTY—Joan Beringer

*P*ARTICULARS *of a light make-up suitable for the seaside.*
  Cardiff. SUNTAN.
  If your skin is greasy use a liquid powder in a suntan shade. This will give your skin a warm outdoor look. Have a lipstick in a vivid shade and groom lashes and brows with a dark ointment.

HOUSEWIFERY—Jennifer Snow

*H*OW *to dye honesty to tone with decoration of room.*
  Gillingham. (MRS.) N.
  Aniline dyes dissolved in methylated spirit are best for this purpose. You can get the dyes in powder form from the arts and crafts department of any big store or from an artists' materials shop. They are usually put up in 6d. boxes. Another pretty effect is obtained by painting the head with gold size and sprinkling with gold, silver, or bronze powder.

CHILDREN AND THE NURSERY—

Sister Cooper, S.R.N.

*M*Y $2\frac{1}{2}$-years-old *daughter drinks a pint of milk and has an egg each day, but does not eat much.*
  Newcastle. (MRS.) B.

  Limit eggs to three a week, giving one for dinner, either coddled or as baked custard, and only give half a pint of milk daily, so that her appetite improves for other necessary food.

DRESS—Victoria Chappelle

I HAVE *an old evening skirt of very heavy satin in good condition. Is there any way of utilising it?*
  Birmingham. (MRS.) L. SALTER.
  Why not make an evening cape of it, cut with two seams on the shoulders or one down the centre of the back? The neck can have a little upstanding stiff collar, a scarf, or a fur trimming.

COOKERY—Doris B. Sheridan

*S*HOULD *extra time be allowed when cooking meat in the oven in a double pan with water in the lower part? Must the water be boiling?*
  London, N.W. R. G.
  No extra time should be required and the water must be hot, not actually boiling, when put into the lower pan.

BEAUTY—Joan Beringer

CAN liquid powder be used without first putting on cream?
Great Barr. WORRIED.

If your skin is dry it is as well to pat in a little cream, which should be wiped off carefully before applying the liquid powder.

CHILDREN AND THE NURSERY —Sister Cooper, S.R.N.

CAN I give undiluted cow's milk to baby aged 9 months?
Stockton-on-Tees. J. L. M.

Undiluted cow's milk should not be given until between 15 and 17 months. The excess of protein is irritating and harmful.

DRESS—Victoria Chappelle

I HAVE bought a piece of plaid woollen material at the sales, but not quite enough to make a frock. Can you tell me how to use it?
London. AUDREY.

Use this for the skirt and make a square panel to button on to a top of plain material just below each shoulder. A belt to match the plain bodice can be used.

HOUSEWIFERY—Jennifer Snow

CAN you suggest a remedy for a creaking floor?
Halifax. (MRS.) PLUMPTON.

The boards have evidently shrunk. Get the gaps filled with thin wedge-shaped pieces glued into position, or fill with a thick paste of plaster of Paris, and then give the boards a coating of linseed oil, rubbing it thoroughly in.

COOKERY—Doris B. Sheridan

A RECIPE for waffles which contains honey.
Taunton. D. M. S.

Work together 4oz. of flour, 1 tablespoonful each of olive oil and orange flower water, 1 egg, and 2½oz. each of water and honey. Cook in waffle-irons in the usual way.

"DAILY MAIL" WOMEN'S BUREAU

BEAUTY—Joan Beringer

MAKE-UP for fair hair going darker, dark eyebrows and lashes, small hazel eyes.
Brighton. VANITY B.

Make your eyes appear larger by carrying the eyeshadow—which can be hazel or brown or green, whichever colour predominates in your eyes—upwards towards the brows and well away from the inner corners of the eyes. Have a pale apricot powder, mandarin rouge and lipstick, and dark brown mascara for your lashes.

HOW to remove hard lumps on the knuckles of the hands.
Muswell Hill. G. J.

Rub the hard skin with powdered pumice, or with a pumice stone dipped in peroxide if the knuckles are discoloured. Massage the fingers with olive oil regularly.

DRESS—Victoria Chappelle

WHAT accessories should I wear with a swagger coat and skirt of drab pink linen?
Cardiff. GRACE.

Dark brown hat, blouse, gloves and shoes with beige stockings will look well; or you might wear a hat in a deeper shade of pink, brown shoes and gloves, beige stockings.

COOKERY—Doris B. Sheridan

RECIPE for a chocolate caramel pudding.
London. (MRS.) K.

Put into a charlotte mould 4oz. caster sugar and 2 tablespoonfuls lemon juice and stand the mould over gentle heat until the sugar is dark brown. Coat this carefully all over the inside of the mould and then fill up with chocolate mixture. To prepare this put 3oz. cut-up chocolate and a good ½-pint milk into a saucepan and cook for about ten minutes over slow heat. Work together 3 eggs, 2 oz. caster sugar, and a few drops vanilla, and add the chocolate mixture, stirring all the time. Pour into the mould and steam slowly for about 1½ hours. Turn out and serve either hot or cold.

CHILDREN AND THE NURSERY— Sister Cooper, S.R.N.

WE are taking baby, now six months old, to the sea this month. How should she bathe?
Bradford. (MRS.) W.

Baby can have a short dip in a sun-warmed pool in your arms, wearing her little bathing suit. Accustom her to a cool sponge now, so that she will be ready to enjoy her bathe.

HOUSEWIFERY—Jennifer Snow

HOW to clean white felt-covered asbestos table-mats which have become discoloured from tea and coffee stains.
Folkestone. JUNE.

Sponge well with hot soapy water in which a little borax has been dissolved.

BEAUTY—Joan Beringer

MY hair has gone very dull and lifeless. Please suggest treatment, also shampoo. I am fair.
Southport. BLUE EYES.

A herbal shampoo, and daily scalp massage, using a tonic lotion made from herbs, will help to restore the hair to good condition. To massage the scalp, press the fingers firmly down and move the scalp in a rotary and up and down movement. Before dressing the hair, brush in a little brightening oil specially made for fair hair.

WHAT make-up to wear with scarlet evening dress? Auburn hair, dark brown eyes, fresh complexion.
Newport. P. E.

For a scarlet evening dress you need a vivid make-up. Have powder of a natural shade, and rouge and lipstick of a shade called Mandarin Rose, with brown eyeshadow and dark brown mascara.

COOKERY—Doris B. Sheridan

TO make onion sauce that will keep white.
Paignton. WONDERING.

Cook together without browning 1 oz. each flour and butter. Add ½ pint white stock or milk and stir over the fire until thick and boiling. Add a tablespoonful of cream, salt and pepper to season, and a finely chopped cooked Spanish onion. Make all hot together.

CHILDREN AND THE NURSERY
—Sister Cooper, S.R.N.

BABY, aged one year and ten months, has so much energy and interest in life that she cannot give enough time to her meals.
Woodbridge. (MRS.) C.

Be very regular with meals, and do not allow any toys or books to come to table. Increase the fresh element, giving a fruit breakfast for 3 or 4 mornings, and so improve her appetite.

HOW can I keep baby's squares a good colour?
Eastbourne. (MRS.) S.

Put the squares in a pail of cold water as soon as they are removed, first rinsing soiled ones. Wash them, using a pure soda-free soap to remove stains, and rinse thoroughly in two waters. Boil them twice a week and dry them out of doors if possible.

DRESS—Victoria Chappelle

I HAVE white hair, which gives me a "washed out" look. What dress colours would remedy this?
Herne Bay. (MISS) W.

Wear rich, deep colours—there are many shades of mauve and wines which would be most becoming to you.

WAY of renovating black and white coat, plain, beltless and about 6in. too short.
Honiton. (MISS) J. C.

Take off the revers, leaving the neck quite plain, and wear a scarf instead. Remove the buttons, replacing them by invisible studs, and add a belt. Or put the buttons higher and make the coat slightly more waisted by taking in the side seams. Cut it to definitely three-quarter length and wear it over a plain black skirt.

HOUSEWIFERY—Jennifer Snow

SUGGESTIONS for making cushions to go with blue carpet and yellow walls.
Stratford. WATENOLATH.

Have blue and amber coloured cushions in artificial slub repp; it wears well and is quite inexpensive.

You will require an inner case of down-proof cambric; this is obtainable 44 inches wide, and costs about 1s. 6d. a yard. Seam up all edges except about 3 inches, and insert the down through this opening by means of a paper funnel. I suggest that you make the covers with one side press studded together, so that they are easily removed for laundering.

HOW can I restore ebony which has turned brown?
Cheltenham. M. L.

Rub in salad oil twice a week for a long period, a treatment which must be patient and continuous.

COOKERY—Doris B. Sheridan

HOW to prepare and serve a prawn and shrimp cocktail.
Glasgow. E. H. G.

Rub the inside of a basin with a clove of garlic, add the required quantities of picked prawns and shrimps, a tablespoonful of tomato ketchup and a few drops of Worcester sauce for each person, with a tiny dust of cayenne. Mix well together, set the bowl on ice and serve in cocktail glasses with a small spoon at each place. Serve rolls of thinly cut buttered brown bread.

NURSERY—Sister Cooper, S.R.N.

MY boy has chilblains on his feet.
Reading. (MRS.) R.

Improve the circulation by regular exercise, such as skipping. Also dip the feet into hot water for 3 minutes, and cold for one minute, alternately.

A course of calcium might be advisable. Rub into the unbroken chilblains a little ointment made from winter-green oil, menthol and olive oil.

DRESS—Victoria Chappelle

I HAVE a lace frock with a small basque, which, when new, flared out all round my waist, but is now very limp. What can I do to stiffen it?
Gloucester. EILEEN.

Sew some fine horsehair lace, about 3in. wide, to match your frock in colour, on the wrong side of the basque. This will stiffen it.

HOUSEWIFERY—Jennifer Snow

HOW should I finish off the edge of oil silk curtains?
Gillingham. E. M. C.

Machine a single fold on this material. This will keep its edges neat and not destroy the hang.

BEAUTY—Joan Beringer

AN inexpensive treatment for removing lines under the eyes and across the forehead.
Monmouth. JUDY.

Olive and almond oils blended in equal parts with a few drops of tincture of benzoin added should be tapped in round the eyes and across the forehead lines every night. Occasionally, lay pads of cotton wool soaked in witch hazel over the eyes and rest them for ten minutes at a time. Visit an oculist.

DRESS—Victoria Chappelle

WOULD it be suitable to wear blue and white sandals with a crêpe-suède frock for a summer wedding? I am rather stout. Can I wear a large hat, and are fishnet gloves and stockings in the same shade right?

London.   (MRS.) W. I. F.

I would suggest plain dark blue or white shoes rather than sandals. A hat with a medium brim and fishnet gloves and stockings in beige should look well.

CHILDREN AND THE NURSERY
—Sister Cooper, S.R.N.

MY three-years-old daughter is never content to be still, even though I punish her.

Netley Abbey.   (MRS.) McK.

Activity is natural, so provide outlet for her energies, and appeal to her sense of responsibility. Let her have a doll to dress and look after, and let her wash its clothes. Give her little jobs to do for you, and let her dress and undress herself. Some gardening tools and a small patch of garden for herself would also help, and she would probably enjoy playing with putty or colour cards, or a sand heap.

BEAUTY—Joan Beringer

TREATMENT for developing the chest.

Whitchurch.   GEM.

Deep breathing is one of the best means of developing the chest measurement. Stand near an open window with the hands stretched in front, palms meeting. Exhale. Expand arms slowly pressing them as far back as possible, at the same time inhaling deeply. Return them to first position, exhaling. Repeat. Practise a similar exercise, but starting with the hands at the sides and raising them above the head until the palms meet. When out walking breathe in rhythmically with each step, counting up to five. Gradually increase this until you can inhale for twelve or more.

COOKERY—Doris B. Sheridan

HOW to use fresh raspberries as a sandwich cake filling.

Sevenoaks.   E. K. F. C.

Split a round sponge sandwich cake, spread each side liberally with sweetened whipped cream and sandwich together with a layer of picked over and sugar sweetened fresh raspberries.

RECIPE for cold meat galantine.

Hale.   M. M.

Remove bones and tendons from a small breast of veal and spread the meat, skin side downwards, on a board. Season with salt, pepper, and grated nutmeg and spread over one pound of sausage-meat. Cover with half pound of lean ham, which has been cut into strips, season with salt and pepper and lay three hard-boiled sliced eggs on top. On this put a second pound of sausage-meat, season, and roll up. Tie in a scalded and floured cloth and put into a pan of boiling water to cover. Simmer for three hours. Stand the roll between two plates until cold, remove the cloth and finish off with glaze or sieved browned bread-crumbs.

HOUSEWIFERY—Jennifer Snow

HOW to clean suède lining of rug.

London.   (MRS.) C.

I think the best thing to do here will be to rub well with fine sandpaper, which will give a new surface to the suède.

HOUSEWIFERY—Jennifer Snow

HOW can I preserve poppy heads?

Birkenhead.   R.

You can leave the heads as they are, thread a wire stem from cap to base, and cover this with green crêpe paper. Paint the head with a cellulose brushing enamel, or paint over with gold size and scatter a metallic powder in gold, silver, or bronze over the surface.

Or soften the heads by plunging into boiling water for a couple of minutes, and then cutting into petals from cap to base with a sharp knife from cap to base. Shape these petals outwards with the hands or stuff the head with soft paper to distend, and put to dry. Then paint or gild as before.

COOKERY—Doris B. Sheridan

A SIMPLE recipe for pressed beef.

Gainford.   (MRS.) H.

Wash and dry a piece of brisket of beef weighing between four and six pounds, rub with a dessertspoonful of mixed spice and rather less salt, and leave overnight. Put into a saucepan of cold water with two bay leaves, a blade of mace, a cut-up carrot and a turnip, a few peppercorns and a little allspice, and simmer gently until the meat will leave the bones easily. Remove the bones and press the meat into a mould or tin. Stand under a weight until cold and set. Brush with melted glaze. The time of cooking should be between two and three hours.

BEAUTY—Joan Beringer

WHAT do you recommend for shine that comes through all powder and face cream, especially on the nose and brow?

Leyland.   WORRIED.

Add 1 per cent. alum to warm water when you wash, carefully bathing the nose and forehead. Try a liquid powder as a powder base.

CHILDREN AND THE NURSERY—
Sister Cooper, S.R.N.

WE have plenty of home-grown vegetables, but I do not buy much meat, and fish disagrees with my boy.

Petersfield.   (MRS.) S.

Give the necessary protein as cheese, nuts, milk, and sometimes egg. Make a protein soup as follows: 2 ounces potatoes and carrots, half an ounce of haricot beans and dried peas, one ounce of dried turnips, and a quart of water. Bring to boil and allow to simmer gently for 4 hours in earthenware pot (or 7lb. jam jar). Unpolished rice or barley can be added and the soup enriched by adding a little milk before serving.

DRESS—Victoria Chappelle

I HAVE a lovely piece of white Chinese silk with bands of embroidery at the borders. How can I make use of it?

Edinburgh.   TAM-O'-SHANTER.

Use this for an afternoon jumper with the bands of embroidery for a small stand-up collar, as belt and on cuffs. If this is made with the opening down one side in the style of a Chinese coat, it will look very effective.

AT your service, the Daily Mail experts will help you with your home, fashion, and beauty problems if you simply write to them enclosing an inquiry form and a stamped addressed envelope for the reply. Address to The Women's Bureau, Northcliffe House, London, E.C. 4, and put the subject of your query on the envelope.

COOKERY—Doris B. Sheridan

IS there a simple remedy for soup that has been made rather too salt?

Bristol.   (MRS.) G. TIMS.

Add a few slices of raw potato to the soup and cook for a few extra minutes.

HOUSEWIFERY—Jennifer Snow

BLEACHING the yellow bristles of hair brushes

Brighton.   E. B.

Let the brushes stand in a shallow tin containing ½ gill of vinegar to 1 pint of warm water. Soak for about 30 minutes. Then rinse in cold water. One part of peroxide of hydrogen to ten parts of warm water may be used once or twice, but its frequent use will rot the bristles.

NURSERY—Sister Cooper, S.R.N.

BABY, aged eight months, is teething. How can I help her?

Wallasey.   (MRS.) W.

Give her a knobbly rubber teething ring. Never press her food if she is disinclined for it, but give extra water, and a little clear fluid magnesia, to cool the blood.

BEAUTY—Joan Beringer

MY complexion is inclined to look grey. What make-up should I use? I have brown hair and hazel eyes. Also what hairdressing? My face is thin.

Anglesey.   DORA.

Have a tinted powder base and keep your powder to the warm apricot tones, with cherry cream rouge and lipstick to tone. Part the hair low on one side with flat waves over the head, but have the sides long enough to curl up over the ears in order to give width to the face.

DRESS—Victoria Chappelle

I HAVE a black coat from which I have taken the fur collar so that it now has a loose round one of material. How can I make this look smart?

Heston.   (MRS.) S. S.

Buy a velvet scarf in a bright shade, such as coral or ruby, and wear it beneath the collar, tying it in front. This will raise the collar against your neck keep you warm, and look chic.

DAILY MAIL WOMEN'S BUREAU
INQUIRY FORM, DEC. 7, 1933.
Pseudonym (if desired) ....
Name ....
Address ....

BEAUTY—Joan Beringer

MY nose is too long, making my chin look receding. How can I dress my hair to balance my chin and nose ?
Faversham.   V. J.

Don't pull your hair over the cheeks but wear it brushed back and curled behind the ears to give a broadening effect. A touch of rouge on the chin under your powder will make this feature more important.

CHILDREN AND THE NURSERY—

Sister Cooper, S.R.N.

THANKS to your special diet, my son's tonsils are reduced, and he is in much better health. What puddings can I give?
Darlington.   (MRS.) G.

Fresh or dried fruit salad or apricot purée, baked apples, or fruit jelly made with fresh fruit juice, or honeycomb

mould. A steamed fruit pudding, using dried fruits, will be good for him in very cold weather.

COOKERY—Doris B. Sheridan

A RECIPE for sand cake.
Cambridge.   (MISS) K.

Beat to a cream 2oz. butter and 4oz. sugar, add two whipped eggs and a few drops of lemon essence, and fold in lightly ½lb. cornflour, 1oz. plain flour and 1 teaspoonful baking powder, which have been sieved together. Bake for about thirty minutes or until nicely browned and risen in a well-buttered and floured cake tin in a moderate oven.

HOUSEWIFERY—Jennifer Snow

TO prevent musty smell in ice box when it is cleaned and put away for the winter.
London.   (MRS.) SHIPTON.

There will be no fustiness if you allow the interior of the box to have a current of air through it Do not shut down the lid; prop it up and arrange a dust sheet over.

DRESS—Victoria Chappelle

I HAVE some pieces of very good monkey-skin. How can I use them?
London.   (MRS.) S. HAINE.

As a " plume " for a hat, as fringing for gauntlet gloves, or a trimming to a collar.

CHILDREN AND THE NURSERY—
Sister Cooper, S.R.N.

*W*E *cannot get our holidays until mid-September, when baby will be five months. Will it be too late for the sea?*
Doncaster. (MRS.) G.

No, but be guided by the weather as to the amount of time you spend on the beach, and go for walks inland if necessary. Do not let baby bathe, but you could pour a little sea water from a sun-warmed pool over her legs if the weather is still sunny.

COOKERY—Doris B. Sheridan

*C*AN *you tell me how to make a yeast Baba?*
Lancaster. T.

Mix ½oz. yeast with 1 tablespoonful caster sugar and ⅛ pint warmed milk and water, and pour into a well in the centre of ⅜lb. warmed flour which has been mixed with a pinch of salt. Make into a batter with some of the flour, draw the remainder over the top and leave to stand in a warm place for 20 minutes. Add 3 large eggs and 5oz. butter and beat thoroughly with the hand.

Put the mixture into a large cake tin, which should be only half full, and set aside in a warm place until the Baba rises to the top of the tin. Bake in a hot oven until a good golden brown colour—rather more than half an hour.

Turn out and soak with syrup made by

:..:
: **INQUIRY FORM, AUG. 21, 1933**
: *DAILY MAIL* WOMEN'S BUREAU
: *Pseudonym (if desired)*
:
: Name ....
:
: Address ....
:..:

boiling ½lb. sugar in 1 pint water with orange or lemon rind to flavour until the mixture reduces to half quantity. The syrup should be used when it is cold. Cut the centre out of the Baba and fill up with layers of custard and fruit. Brush the sides with warmed apricot jam

and cover with shredded almonds. Garnish the top with whipped cream, red currant jelly, and glacé fruits.

A RECIPE *for making shrimps into an appetising sandwich filling.*

Pound and sieve quarter-pint picked shrimps, two boned anchovies, and 4oz. butter with salt and pepper to season.

BEAUTY—Joan Beringer

I HAVE *a coarse skin with open pores round chin and at the corners of the nose.*
Matlock. S. W.

Instead of soap, use a gritty cream for washing. This will stimulate the sluggish condition of the skin and help to refine

---

Queries must be accompanied by a **STAMPED ADDRESSED ENVELOPE** and an inquiry form. Write the subject—whether dress, children, cookery, housewifery, or beauty—at the top left-hand corner of the envelope and address it to:
" Daily Mail " Women's Bureau, Northcliffe House, London, E.C. 4.

the pores. Avoid greasy foods and **try** to do five minutes exercise daily.

I HAVE *to wash my face in hard water and my skin gets very dry.*
Bury St. Edmunds. G.

There is no necessity to wash in hard water. Add a pinch of borax to the water, or, better still, leave some lemon or orange peel in a jug overnight and your washing water will be deliciously soft and fragrant in the morning. Until your skin improves, wash the face as little as possible. Cleanse instead with almond and olive oil in equal parts.

HOUSEWIFERY—Jennifer Snow

*H*OW *to clean a copper kettle which is burnt black.*
Bury St. Edmunds. B.

Before attempting to remove the black, leave the kettle wrapped in rags soaked in paraffin overnight. Then a scouring with a soap powder and paraffin should bring it into condition.

*C*AN *I make table napkins into cloths?*
Dover. D.

I think your idea of joining the napkins to make afternoon cloths is excellent. Use Cluny lace and insertion—this is made in linen threads and in bold designs and will wear as long as the linen cloth.

DRESS—Victoria Chappelle

I AM *having a jacket made for autumn wear outdoors. Should it be waist length?*
Bournemouth. PAULINA.

No; have it made about 6in. below the hip-line, for this is the newest length.

*H*OW *can I make use of some ostrich feathers?*
Ealing. ECONOMICAL.

Wear them in a little velvet toque. They should be small feathers, gathered into a close bunch.

BEAUTY—Joan Beringer

*H*OW *to bring back the yellow tint and healthy gloss to my fair hair, which a bad " perm " has made brittle and dull. Olive oil makes it darker.*
Accrington M. P.

Try odourless castor oil. Rub well into the scalp and leave on for some hours before washing. Get a dry scalp tonic, and give it a daily massage with five minutes' extra brushing at night. If the hair has been badly burnt you will have to wait until it has grown out.

COOKERY—Doris B. Sheridan

*W*HAT *is a Bavaroise?*
London. M. K.

A custard set with gelatine so that it can be turned out of its mould.

NURSERY—Sister Cooper, S.R.N.

*S*UITABLE *winter clothing for two-years-old boy.*
Cowes. (MRS.) W.

Long-sleeved vest and warm material bodice, to which is buttoned the warm, washable lining to his knickers. These can be of serge or corduroy, and he could wear a jersey with them.

DRESS—Victoria Chappelle

*W*HAT *to wear with a plaid skirt?*
Eye. L. S.

A jacket in the predominant colour of the skirt in velvet, or supple wool, with a cream silk or tussore blouse.

HOUSEWIFERY—Jennifer Snow

A REMEDY *for removing clear spots from an oxidised silver fire curb.*
Camborne. CURB.

Try rubbing the curb with a solution of sulphate of soda in warm water —1oz. to 1 pint. Dissolve the soda in boiling water and use when only warm. This ought to remove any ordinary marks, but, if the clear spots have been caused by any acid, I think resilvering will be necessary.

BEAUTY—Joan Beringer

IS it correct to grease the eyelids? And will vaseline make the eyelashes grow?
    WORRIED.
    Kingston-on-Thames.

Oiled eyelids are very fashionable just now, and vaseline can be used for the purpose quite effectively. It can also be applied with advantage to the eyelashes, but in both cases should be used sparingly.

THE *Daily Mail* Women's Bureau has solved thousands of problems, and is ready to help YOU. Write to the expert concerned at the *Daily Mail* Women's Bureau, Northcliffe House, London, E.C. 4—and don't forget to enclose a stamped addressed envelope and an inquiry form

DRESS—Victoria Chappelle

HOW can I use some yellow and brown checked material roughly one yard square?
    Swansea.   I. W.

As a shoulder yoke and upper sleeves on a plain brown or yellow frock, or as scarf and handbag with a brown or yellow outfit.

NURSERY— Sister Cooper, S.R.N.

MY six-years-old son has just returned from the scarlet fever hospital. Please give some hints for his convalescence.
    Waterbeach.   (MRS.) S.

Give an easily digested yet nourishing diet, and ensure ample fresh air. Try to provide congenial and interesting occupation without enforcing lessons or "work" of any kind against his will. A midday rest with a book would be advisable, as any over-fatigue must be avoided in order to prevent heart strain, to which a person recovering from scarlet fever is predisposed.

HOUSEWIFERY—Jennifer Snow

HOW to clean a natural colour sheep-skin rug.
    Ashurst.   POP.

Wash the rug; remove the lining and wash it separately. Choose a bright breezy day, and let the skin soak for an hour or two in a pail or tub of water to which household ammonia has been added—a tablespoonful to every pail of water. Poke and press the rug about—a hand vacuum washer is excellent for this purpose—until most of the dirt is extracted. Then put into another tub of warm water with more ammonia, and wash very thoroughly. Rinse in two or three clean waters, and, if you can, put through the wringer. If not hang the rug out to drip dry; then shake frequently during the final drying process. When perfectly dry, comb the fleece with a steel comb.

COOKERY—Doris B. Sheridan

WILL you kindly tell me how to serve sheep's tongues in glass as a hot dish?
    Hampstead.   BETTY.

The tongues could be made hot in the following sauce and served with peas and potatoes or a macedoine of mixed vegetables. For the sauce, cook together without browning an ounce each of flour and butter, add ½-pint milk salt and pepper to season, a cut-up onion and a bag of herbs, and simmer until the onion is tender. Take out the herbs, rub the sauce through a sieve, add two tablespoonfuls of cream or unsweetened tinned milk, and a dust of nutmeg, and re-heat with the tongues.

DRESS—Victoria Chappelle

HOW can I brighten up a plain black wool frock with a throat-high neckline? I am tired of ordinary collars.
    Dublin.   ISOBEL.

Make two or three "necklace" collars in red, green, turquoise blue, or coral. These should be cut from strips of bias material about 6in. or 7in. wide, so that they drape themselves round the neck. Have the edge picoted, and after twisting the collar round the neck, button the ends on to the dress below each shoulder in front.

NURSERY—Sister Cooper, S.R.N.

BABY, aged 11 months, cannot take orange juice. Can I give tomato instead?
    London.   (MRS.) T.

Yes, either raw tomato or raw swede juice can be given. The juice should be strained and diluted with warm water. Have you tried to give the juice of the very sweet oranges which are now obtainable?

HOUSEWIFERY—Jennifer Snow

WHAT aniline dye is used for colouring pressed beech leaves, and how is it sold?
    Sonning.   M. E. TURNER.

Aniline dyes are sold in powder form in 6d. boxes in the crafts departments of most of the big stores. A mixture of scarlet and sienna gives a good rich colour. Dissolve the powder in methylated spirit very thoroughly, and dip the leaves into it.

COOKERY—Doris B. Sheridan

PLEASE repeat last year's Christmas pudding recipe. It was so good.
    Cardiff.   (MRS.) K. W.

Mix together 1½lb. shredded suet, 1lb. Demerara sugar, 1lb. each sultanas and raisins, 4oz. each shredded citron peel and candied peel, 1 chopped russet apple, 1 teaspoonful mixed spice, half a grated nutmeg, 2 teaspoonfuls salt, 1lb. sieved breadcrumbs, and 8oz. plain flour. Add 1lb. whipped eggs (weighed in their shells), ½ pint new milk, and a wineglassful of brandy, and stir all together until thoroughly blended. Cover with a clean cloth and set aside in a cool place for twelve hours. Divide into buttered moulds or basins and boil steadily for eight hours or steam for nine hours.

BEAUTY—Joan Beringer

WHAT colour powder and lip rouge could I use for the day-time? Medium complexion, brown eyes, and red-brown hair.
    Headington.   E. C.

Have rouge and lipstick of rather a bright shade with a definite orange tone.

COOKERY—Doris B. Sheridan

RECIPES for cool drinks made from cherries and raspberries.
    Blackpool.   P.

Cherryade. — Crush 1lb. picked-over cherries and break a few of the stones. Put the fruit into a saucepan with the kernels and 1 pint of water, bring to the boil and boil steadily for five minutes. Sieve, stir in 3oz. sugar, and when cold store in bottles. Serve two tablespoonfuls diluted with each tumbler of water or soda water.

Raspberry Syrup.—Boil 8oz. sugar and ½ pint water for five minutes, add 1 pint raspberry juice, and simmer for about three-quarters of an hour, removing any scum that rises. Bottle when cold and serve diluted with water or soda water.

CHILDREN AND THE NURSERY—Sister Cooper, S.R.N.

MY four-years-old daughter is energetic and high-spirited, but possesses a very bad temper.
    Kensal Rise.   (MRS.) B.

Be sure that she has ample outlet for her energies. Send her to a nursery school, if possible; give scope for her independence, letting her dress herself, lay the table at meals, and "help" you generally. Try to avoid undue thwarting, and give as few commands as possible, always leading her by cheerful suggestion. Be very calm and patient yourself.

BEAUTY—Joan Beringer

MAKE-UP for a blonde. Slight hint of red in the hair; green-grey eyes and good skin.
    Morden.   ENQUIRER.

Tangerine rouge and lipstick and pale apricot powder would be attractive with your colouring. Bring out the green in your eyes by wearing green eyeshadow. By day use a mid-brown mascara, but at night you should be able to wear the new green mascara with striking effect.

WHAT quantity of boric powder to use as a wash for the eyes?
    Methuen Park.   M.

Dissolve a teaspoonful in a tumbler of hot water and allow to cool. Or a tiny pinch to an eye cup of warm water.

HOW to get rid of a double chin.
    London, N.W.   BEEBER.

Daily massage and a few minutes' exercise will help to improve the contour. Place the fingers of both hands at the back of the neck and with the thumbs massage the chin across and upwards towards the ears. Practise this exercise. Throw the head back and slowly open and shut the mouth. Then rotate the head from left to right and right to left with slow lolling movements.

HOUSEWIFERY—Jennifer Snow

Perfume stains are very difficult to remove, for they are partly spirit and partly oil. I suggest that you sponge the stain first with methylated spirit and warm water—equal parts. Then sponge with a non-inflammable cleaning liquid.

DRESS—Victoria Chappelle

PLEASE suggest frocks for twin bridesmaids of seven years and an older girl of 17.
    Birmingham.   E. W.

Lavender organdi for the older girl's frock made simply, with a skirt cut to fit over the hips then gradually fuller towards hem, with a little cape or jacket. A wreath of pale delicate green leaves on her head and a posy of flowers in her frock colour or a little muff in organdi would look well. The children's frocks, in the same shade or a pale pink to tone, might have round necks, puff sleeves and flounces round the hem of the skirts. Bronze shoes.

"DAILY MAIL" WOMEN'S BUREAU

FIVE experts are ready to solve YOUR problems! Write to-day—and remember to enclose with your inquiry form a stamped addressed envelope! Only a very small proportion of the hundreds of letters received can be printed—the rest are answered by post. Address to the "Daily Mail" Women's Bureau, Northcliffe House, London, E.C. 4, marking the topic—whether cookery, beauty, children, housewifery, or dress—at the top left-hand corner of the envelope.

COOKERY—Doris B. Sheridan

RECIPE for lambs' tongues cooked in a casserole.
Herne Hill. E. H. C.

Wash and blanch the tongues, put them into a buttered casserole with sliced mixed vegetables, mixed herbs, peppercorns, and mace, and cook over quick heat for ten minutes. Add about a pint of stock, set the lid on the casserole, and cook until tender—about two hours.

Take up the tongues, remove the skins, cut each into two portions lengthwise, and brush over with glaze. Reheat in the oven and dish on a potato purée border, pouring the strained and thickened gravy round.

My lemon marmalade set when I made it, but has now turned soft. Can I re-boil it?
Sunderland. (Miss) S.

You evidently did not boil your marmalade sufficiently fast after the sugar was added. Without adding either sugar or water, re-boil it for a few minutes until a little of the preserve, when tested on a saucer, will set well.

Why did cream buns made from choux pastry collapse when taken from the oven, and have stodgy centres?
Gloucester. J. D.

Because the oven was not sufficiently hot. Choux pastry requires a hot oven, and éclairs and cream buns should take about half an hour to cook.

BEAUTY—Joan Beringer

SUGGEST thorough face-cleansing treatment. I use cold water, but this makes my face sore.
Risca. S. D. H.

The face should be washed in warm water, not cold, at night. To prevent its becoming sore, cleanse before washing with cleansing cream or almond oil. Wipe off; apply a second coating, then wash the face thoroughly, using a pure unscented soap. Massage with nourishing cream, and in the morning rinse the face with cold water softened by adding a few drops of eau de Cologne.

My hair is white, dry, and inclined to be frizzy. Would a permanent wave take out the natural wave?
Rye. (Mrs.) S.

A permanent wave, especially in the case of white hair, would tend to increase the frizziness. The scalp should be well massaged with warm olive oil before shampooing and the hair then water-waved. A net should be worn for sleeping, and a little brilliantine brushed in when dressing the hair.

When I use white or cream powder, tiny thread veins show through and give a purple effect.
Muswell Hill. (Mrs.) H.

As you are dark, use a tinted foundation cream and a pinky natural powder, with a cream rouge of rather a dark shade. Work this well into the skin and blend it carefully. At night a little mauve or jade powder added to the ordinary powder will detract from the high colour.

DRESS—Victoria Chappelle

SUGGEST alterations to black spring coat which seems dowdy. It is unbelted and has long revers and turned down collar worked with braid to match sleeve-ends.
Burnage. (MRS.) F. C. GRIFFITHS.

Make it slightly waisted by taking in side seams a little and putting a couple of darts at back. Remove braid from collar and cuffs, afterwards pressing well. Add wide black suède, leather or stitched self-material belt, with plain, smart buckle.

I have a length of Black Watch tartan. How can I use it?
Belfast. WONDERING.

Have a frock made of it, and wear it with a full-length wool crêpe navy coat. A tartan scarf and a navy beret trimmed with a tartan tab will complete a good outfit.

Spring or summer outfit for 16-years-old girl, who looks older.
Queenborough. MICKY.

Long navy princess coat over patterned frock (navy and white or similar alliance) for summer. Grey suit with dark jumper, say blue; or navy suit with lighter blue jumper.

My hip-length suède jacket is much too narrow.
Newport. M. E. M.

Make a waistcoat front of matching suède or thin rough woollen material in same green, fastening with buttons. If you cannot attach this to the side seams of jacket, put a couple of straps at waist to fasten at the back, with a loop at the top to pass behind your neck. The jacket can remain open or be buttoned on to the waistcoat.

What to wear with black, white, green and red herringbone tweed jacket.
Wroughton. (Miss) J. E. COXON.

Your own idea of a green wrap-over skirt is quite good. You can make alliance with the coat by collar, cuffs, and belt of the same green.

CHILDREN & THE NURSERY— Sister Cooper, S.R.N.

HOW to prevent a baby from turning on his face when sleeping.
Harrow. F. L. B.

Provide a chaff pillow, and, until the habit is overcome, use webbing shoulder straps. Make sure feeding is correct, as to lie on the face sometimes indicates indigestion.

When is baby's 10 p.m. feed discontinued?
Eccles. (MRS.) B.

This feed is decreased at 10 months and discontinued by the first birthday, though some babies progress well on four feeds a day earlier than this.

Approximate hours of sleep required by children between 6 and 15 years.
Leamington. ANXIOUS.

A child of six years needs 12 hours, nine years 11 hours, twelve years 10½ hours, fifteen years 9 hours.

I have difficulty in controlling my daughter at times; she seems to need a good old-fashioned spanking!
Herts. JOHN BLUNT.

There are two opinions on the "spanking" question. I myself feel that there are other more satisfactory ways of maintaining discipline. To smack does not encourage self-control or independence, or enable the child to act rightly when there is no one to smack her. You are representing yourself as one who inflicts pain, not one who understands the activities and interests of a child. Remember the force of example, and do not fix your standard too high for the child's age.

Directions for making a sheath for protruding ears.
Catford. (MRS.) E.

Choose a wide mesh net and have a band in front, passing over the top of baby's head, down over the ears, and fastening under his chin. The cap should be worn only at night.

INQUIRY FORM, February 22, 1933
DAILY MAIL WOMEN'S BUREAU
Pseudonym (if desired).

....

Name ....

Address ....

....

HOUSEHOLD HINTS ABC

from Jennifer Snow's Postbag

ALABASTER light bowls that have become yellow can be whitened if you dust very carefully, then wash in warm soapy water to which you have added an equal quantity of hydrogen peroxide. Rinse in clear warm water, and dry well. The bowl must not be allowed to stay in the water. Lay it on the table and wash by rubbing with a wet flannel.

BLACK CHARMALAINE which has become shiny can be improved by sponging with a cloth wrung tightly out of dark blue water. Rub over with a dry cloth and press on the wrong side with a moderate iron.

COCO MATTING can be cleaned, even when very dirty and stained, with hot soapy water and a dash of ammonia. Use 1 tablespoonful of ammonia to 1 quart of water.

LIME can sometimes be prevented from clogging household pipes if a fur collector—a piece of loofah—is kept in the tank and renewed from time to time.

OIL PAINTINGS which are dry and cracked should be rubbed with refined linseed oil. A very little of the oil is required at a time, and it must be completely rubbed in, otherwise the action of the air causes it to solidify which will ruin the appearance of the paintings.

SOCKS which have shrunk should be soaked in lukewarm water for 10 minutes, using 1oz. of borax to 1 gallon of water. Then wash by squeezing in lukewarm soapy water till clean. Do not rub any part of the sock. Rinse in lukewarm water, and put through the wringer till no more moisture can be extracted. Put to dry in a warm place, but not too close to fire.

WINDOW LEATHERS should be soaked, when new, for 10 minutes in lukewarm water and vinegar—¼ gill of vinegar to 1 quart of water. Rinse in lukewarm water, squeeze in lukewarm soapy water, rinse in another soapy water, press in a cloth till no more moisture can be extracted, put to dry in a warm place, and when nearly dry pull gently on the cross and rub between the hands. On future occasions, omit the steeping in vinegar, using the soapy water treatment only.

The Week's Fashion Note

That Feathery Touch

EVERY Paris dress show features feathers in some original form. Here you see some of them.

For instance—at the top left—there is a fine straw turban with a close mass of tiny ostrich tips at the back to give that high line so fashionable just now. The collarette is composed of similar tips arranged in two regular rows, curled in towards the centre and mounted on a satin ribbon that ties at one side.

A beret made of small iridescent breast-feathers, starting in the centre of the top, is shown in the lower sketch. The close-fitting collar, also of breast feathers, ties at the back with a bow of midnight-blue velvet ribbon.

At the right you see the unusual sleeve-trimming of a new cocktail-frock—a double row of marabout tips.